BLOCKCHAIN
LOYALTY

First published in 2019 by Loyalty & Reward Co Pty Ltd

National Library of Australia Cataloguing in-Publication entry:

Creator: Shelper, Philip, author.

Title: Blockchain Loyalty: Disrupting loyalty and reinventing marketing using blockchain and cryptocurrencies (2nd edition)/ Philip Shelper.

ISBN: 978-0-6483535-3-9 (paperback) Ingram Spark

978-0-6483535-5-3 (ebook)

Subjects: blockchain loyalty

cryptocurrency loyalty

blockchain marketing

loyalty programs

Printed by Ingram Spark.

Cover design by Damonza.

Editorial services by Stacey Lyons and Max Savransky.

Diagrams by Stacey Lyons.

Disclaimer

BLOCKCHAIN
LOYALTY

DISRUPTING **LOYALTY** AND REINVENTING **MARKETING** USING **BLOCKCHAIN** AND **CRYPTOCURRENCIES**

PHILIP SHELPER

WITH CONTRIBUTIONS BY **PIPER ALDERMAN**

2ND EDITION

TABLE OF CONTENTS

For the Shelpers and the Irelands; my two families.

INTRODUCTION

Blockchain can be applied to loyalty programs in two main ways:

- **Cryptocurrency Rewards:** A blockchain loyalty program rewards members for their spend with a cryptocurrency (or cryptotoken) instead of traditional points and miles. The cryptocurrency can be actively traded on a digital exchange, similar to a Forex exchange, meaning the value can fluctuate. Thus, rather than holding a balance of points and miles where the value remains static, the member holds a new type of digital currency with a value which constantly adjusts based on speculative investor behaviour and the market forces of supply and demand. The loyalty currency itself becomes a game; one of acquiring, holding and trading. The potential exists to drive much deeper member engagement with a cryptocurrency than with points and miles as members can become fascinated with the idea of earning a currency which is 'alive'. Variations of this model exist, where the cryptotoken value remains static but the program allows members to easily transfer cryptotokens between different programs to unlock value.

- **Enterprise Blockchain Loyalty Solutions:** A blockchain platform can be integrated with a loyalty platform and retail partner platforms to facilitate secure, real-time, auto-reconciled transactions. This approach provides specific advantages for major loyalty programs which have large, expensive legacy systems. While the legacy systems can process enormous volumes of transactions with high stability, they are often inflexible, limiting the ability of the loyalty program operators to innovate. Back-end blockchain platforms connect to the system and allow campaign rules to be exported, meaning the operator can more easily execute complex campaigns without having to develop or replace their legacy platform. They also allow for easier on-boarding of partners where members can earn or redeem points and miles, and more efficient processing of transactions, reducing administrative overheads. The approach focuses specifically on the application of blockchain solutions, with cryptocurrencies only used if the existing loyalty currency requires tokenisation to improve transactional processing efficiencies.

Blockchain Loyalty provides deep insight into how the new technology of blockchain is being used to disrupt loyalty and reinvent marketing around the world by exploring five main areas. The first four areas fall under Cryptocurrency Loyalty, while the fifth area falls under Enterprise Blockchain Loyalty Solutions:

1. A loyalty program powered by a single new cryptotoken

2. A loyalty program powered by an existing cryptocurrency

3. Many loyalty programs powered by multiple new cryptotokens on a single platform

4. A security token supported by a loyalty program

5. A loyalty program enhanced by an enterprise blockchain loyalty solution

Blockchain delivers the biggest opportunity in the past 30 years for companies to gain a competitive edge with new loyalty program approaches. If successful, the result will be more loyal customers, increased sales, a more responsive marketing database, genuine market differentiation and significant profits.

This area is so new that at the time of writing there are no blockchain loyalty programs using cryptocurrencies or cryptotokens operating in the world at scale, although a small number of major loyalty programs are now using enterprise blockchain loyalty solutions.

This 2nd Edition has been released just nine months after the launch of the 1st Edition in June 2018. During that time a protracted bear market has decimated the value of the majority of cryptocurrencies and cryptotokens, with many seeing value plunges in excess of 98% from their peaks, with reserve valuations being all but eliminated. This has dramatically affected the landscape for blockchain loyalty programs, both existing and planned. The demise of Initial Coin offerings (ICO's) is making it incredibly hard for start-up blockchain loyalty programs to raise the necessary funds to launch much more than just a promise. With the irrational exuberance removed, the ability to see the true opportunities for blockchain loyalty is much clearer and the future still appears bright for the use of blockchain in loyalty programs.

The magnitude of the impact blockchain and cryptocurrencies will have on the loyalty industry will only be evident after several years. Future editions of this book will detail the successes and failures of different approaches to better illustrate the optimal applications of blockchain loyalty. Advances will be detailed regularly on *www.blockchainloyalty.io*, a global resource centre for blockchain loyalty.

It is certainly an exciting and dynamic space to be immersed in, and one which offers enormous potential for the loyalty industry.

CHAPTER 1
WHAT IS BLOCKCHAIN AND CRYPTOCURRENCY?

To COMPREHEND WHAT this book will delve into, a brief overview of the fundamentals of blockchain and cryptocurrency is required. Here's a simple example of how a blockchain transaction works:

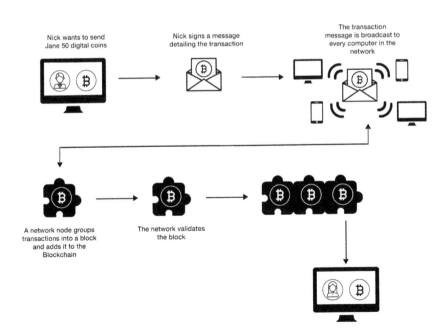

HOW A BLOCKCHAIN TRANSACTION WORKS

Nick wants to send Jane 50 digital coins

Nick signs a message detailing the transaction

The transaction message is broadcast to every computer in the network

A network node groups transactions into a block and adds it to the Blockchain

The network validates the block

A blockchain is a continuously growing list of records, called 'blocks', which are cryptographically secured and linked into a 'chain'. Blockchains are inherently resistant to modification of the data because the data in all the blocks must match in order for a record to be valid and the blocks are held by millions of computers around the world. Blocks are a ledger which aren't controlled by a central entity, hence the term 'decentralised ledger technology' or DLT. The 'millions of computers around the world' are run by Miners. Miners use special software to solve math problems and are rewarded with *cryptocurrency* bonuses. This creates an incentive for more people to mine, increasing the network size and expanding the decentralisation and security of the blockchain platform.

Because blockchain is so secure, it allows for the creation of a trustworthy digital currency, or cryptocurrency, without the need for a centralised authority (such as a bank or loyalty program) to maintain a ledger. Prior to blockchain, a decentralised digital currency couldn't be trusted because there was no way for the holder to ascertain whether it had already been spent or not. Blockchain solves this problem because a transaction creates a decentralised, immutable record stored on the blockchain for everyone to see, making it easy to verify who the actual owner of the cryptocurrency is.

In the blockchain world, there are *cryptocurrencies* and there are *cryptotokens*. The difference is subtle but important. Cryptocurrencies are the core currency of a blockchain platform and are used to reward Miners for creating blocks. Examples include Bitcoin (BTC), Ethereum (ETH) and NEO (NEO). Cryptotokens are digital assets which are issued on top of a blockchain platform. For example, SophiaTX have their SPHTX token hosted on Ethereum platform. Unlike cryptocurrencies, the control of cryptotokens is held on a private ledger maintained by an individual company. This means the company can create a set amount of tokens and make all the decisions about how they are distributed, which allows for a variety of different applications. Specifically, for a loyalty program it provides the opportunity to create a new type of loyalty currency with an inherent utility and value. Both cryptocurrencies and cryptotokens can be used to power blockchain loyalty programs, each providing different advantages which will be explored extensively in the book.

The first blockchain was launched in 2009, supported by a paper titled

Bitcoin: A Peer-to-Peer Electronic Cash System by Satoshi Nakamoto[1]. Nakamoto has since been discovered to be a pseudonym and debate has raged ever since about who they are. (For the essential history of Bitcoin read *Digital Gold* by Nathaniel Popper).

Since then, a large number of blockchain platforms have been developed with different capabilities. Here's a short list of some key players and what their platforms do:

Ethereum: allows for the running of smart contracts, applications that run without downtime, third party interference and censorship. It supports interesting uses such as registries of debts and the moving of funds once certain criteria are reached (smart contracts).

Ripple: connects banks, payment providers, digital asset exchanges and corporates via RippleNet to send money globally in real time with minimal transaction fees.

Nxt: supports the financial technology, crowdfunding and governance industries by providing a modular toolset to build with.

NEM: a permissioned private blockchain delivering industry leading transaction rates for internal ledgers. Its consensus mechanism and the super-node program ensure that it can grow without compromising throughput or stability.

NEO: a non-profit community based blockchain project that utilises blockchain technology and digital identity to digitise and automate the management of digital assets using smart contracts and create a smart economy with a distributed network. On the NEO blockchain, users are able to register, trade and circulate multiple types of assets.

Hyperledger: an open source collaborative effort created to advance cross industry blockchain technologies. It is a global collaboration, hosted by The Linux Foundation, comprised of leaders in finance, banking, Internet of Things (IoT), supply chains, manufacturing and technology.

Red Belly Blockchain: the fastest blockchain platform in the world (at the time of writing). It offers unprecedented throughput of more than six hundred thousand transactions per second (an order of magnitude faster than Visa). Its safety aspect is of invaluable importance for critical industries, like banking and offers performance that scales horizontally.

---

1 https://bitcoin.org/bitcoin.pdf

Essentially, blockchain is about *trust*. The only way a record on a block can be altered is if all records on that block stored in all the computers in the network are altered simultaneously. If the record held by one computer differs to that held by the rest of the computers, it will be rejected. Blockchain is digital democracy in action.

For a large blockchain system containing millions of computers, hacking a block, altering the data on it and having the data accepted by the network is deemed impossible, particularly when the data on each block is protected by heavy cryptographic algorithms. This all makes for an incredibly secure and trustworthy system.

What does this level of trust allow companies to do which they couldn't do in the past? Let's look at some examples:

Chai Wine Vault

The Chai Wine Vault ensures the value and protection of fine wine investments. The vault secures a fine wine's provenance and authenticity in an immutable digital ledger on Everledger's blockchain platform. Everledger's raison d'être is to be a digital global ledger that tracks and protects items of value.

To authenticate a bottle, The Chai Method collects 90+ data points, high resolution photography and records of a bottle's ownership and storage. Everledger uses this data to produce a unique, digital thumbprint of the bottle that is written permanently into Hyperledger.

This digital proof travels with the wine as it moves between the different stakeholders in the wine supply chain, with ownership and storage records updated as the bottle changes hands.

Licensed retailers, warehouses, auction houses and other sale platforms can link to the bottle's digital identity to verify provenance resulting in an increase of the asset's value.

According to Chai Wine Vault, counterfeit bottles account for an estimated 20 per cent of international wine sales. They've increasingly become a problem in the fine wine industry, with the most famous fraudster Rudy Kurniawan reportedly selling over US$150 million in counterfeit bottles before he was caught.[2]

---

2 https://www.theguardian.com/global/2016/sep/11/

Prior to the invention of the blockchain and its application to wine security, only the formal reporting of an authenticator could prove a bottle of wine was counterfeit. Certifying a bottle as authentic was impossible given the risk of document tampering and the inability for the certificate to stay connected with the wine as it changed ownership and location.

Blockchain has thus delivered trust in fine wine.

Diamond Vault

Everledger is also being used to track and protect diamonds. Working with major certification houses around the globe, Everledger successfully created a digital thumbprint for individual diamonds. Everledger also incorporated the Kimberley Process into their system— a certification scheme launched in 2000 which imposes extensive requirements in the process of rough diamond production to prevent the occurrence of blood diamonds; stones sources from conflict areas and used to fund wars.

Now, when diamonds are bought and sold, buyers can verify their provenance and the legitimacy of ownership by verifying them with Everledger. With over 1,000,000 stones registered, this makes life much more difficult for those trying to illegally profit from diamonds.

Blockchain has thus delivered trust in diamonds.

Power Ledger

In Perth, Australia, blockchain is being applied to the energy sector to create a new market for excess solar generated electricity.

Power Ledger uses blockchain technology to enable households and buildings to trade excess solar power peer to peer to make power more distributed and sustainable for consumers. The Power Ledger system tracks the generation and consumption of all trading participants and settles energy trades on predetermined terms and conditions in near real time.

A household can sell their excess solar energy to their neighbour in exchange for a cryptocurrency called Sparkz. This is an alternative method of selling it back into the grid where the local energy company will pay a fraction of the price they sell it to other consumers for. Effectively, Power Ledger is

the-great-wine-fraud-a-vintage-swindle

cutting out the middleman and allowing ordinary consumers to trade electricity with each other for a higher profit.

Blockchain has thus delivered trust in peer to peer energy sales.

LOOMIA

The LOOMIA Electronic Layer (LEL) is a soft flexible circuit with the ability to sense changes, such as heat and touch, in its environment and can be embedded into textiles and garments. It can be paired with the LOOMIA Tile, which captures the garments' usage data and then sends it to the LOOMIA Data Exchange, a blockchain platform which stores the unique data against the user's profile. That data can then be sold by the user or exchanged for rewards.

The challenge for most garment manufacturers is that once they've sold a garment, they have no way of tracking what happens to it. This poses all kinds of implications from marketing to product quality to standard research. The manufacturer could ask the user to fill in a diary and return the garment after some time for analysis, but this proves to be an unreliable source of information.

LOOMIA technology solves this problem. As an example, Nike may choose in the future to incorporate LEL into their shoes. As the shoes are used by the complicit customer, the data is automatically captured by the LOOMIA Tile and then sent to the LOOMIA Data Exchange. The customer can exchange their usage data, as well as demographic data, with Nike in exchange for a reward such as a discount voucher on their next pair of Nikes. Nike now has a very rich data set to explore the different ways in which their shoes are used once they leave the store, an insight they've never had before.

Blockchain has thus delivered trust in product usage data collection.

IBM Blockchain

IBM have teamed up with Walmart to bring safety and assurance to the food supply chain. By utilising blockchain technology, the provenance of a food item can be tracked all the way from the farm (or the manufacturer) to the store and the home.

The most immediate opportunity for this new application is to track down contaminated products which require recall. Food contamination can be costly for both the companies involved and the consumer. Being able to accurately track down all products from a specific batch means faster response times, which can save lives. It also means lower costs because the uncontaminated products aren't also destroyed unnecessarily.

Blockchain has thus delivered trust to the food supply chain.[3]

Blockchain is very new technology and just like the myriad of issues which existed when the internet was first evolving, there are a number of current user challenges.

Transaction times can be lengthy and are sometimes expensive. The transaction processing capacity per second of many blockchain platforms is a fraction of that generated by major systems such as Visa and Mastercard. This is set to change however, with new platforms such as EOS reportedly processing 1,200-4,000 transactions per second (tps) and Ethereum 2.0 due for release late 2019 set to ramp up that platform's tps significantly.

Setting up to trade cryptocurrencies can be complicated. A user needs to open an exchange account and transfer fiat currency in (such as US dollars, British pounds or Australian dollars), which takes days. They then need to open accounts with other exchanges to access the particular cryptocurrency or cryptotoken they wish to trade. They're told not to keep currency in exchanges because they can be hacked or go bankrupt, so they need to create a wallet and transfer their cryptocurrency across or store them on a hard wallet (an advanced USB drive). Private keys for wallets are long, and if the key is lost the wallet can never be opened and the cryptocurrency is locked away forever.

When selling coins or tokens, withdrawing funds from an exchange can also take a long time because most exchanges limit the amount which can be withdrawn each day.

Additionally, when things go wrong, it is often difficult to access support. Exchanges generally don't have phone support and responses to emails can take days or months. In early 2019, the CEO of Canadian exchange QuadrigaCX died, taking with him to his grave the private keys to a cold wallet which stored US$190 million of cryptocurrencies held on behalf of investors. With no one else having access to the keys, they cryptocurrencies are inaccessible. On report estimated 17 to 23 per cent of Bitcoin is already lost.[3]

---

3 *https://www.pymnts.com/blockchain/bitcoin/2017/bitcoin-cryptocurrency-value-lost/*

Certainly, the useability of blockchain and cryptocurrencies has a long way to go to ensure it is easily accessible and provides a seamless customer experience. There are many companies and individuals working on solving these problems to open up to more mass market appeal. A blockchain loyalty program providing cryptocurrencies or cryptotokens as rewards has a significant role to play in supporting mainstream usage of blockchain and cryptocurrencies by implementing a middle layer between the member and the platform which delivers rapid transactions, an intuitive customer experience and accessible support.

CHAPTER 2

A SHORT HISTORY OF LOYALTY PROGRAM CURRENCIES

To UNDERSTAND THE potential roles cryptocurrencies and cryptotokens can play in a loyalty program, it's essential to review different loyalty currencies and their uses throughout history.

As discussed in Chapter 1, prior to blockchain decentralised digital currencies couldn't be trusted because there was no way for the holder to ascertain whether it had already been spent or not. Now, there are several thousand cryptocurrencies and cryptotokens. For the first time in history it is possible for someone (other than a king, emperor, pharaoh, sultan or government official) to create a valuable and usable currency and build its value into billions of dollars.

What opportunity does this create for loyalty programs? With cryptocurrencies and cryptotokens, loyalty program providers now have an alternative to rewarding their members with loyalty points or miles. A review of the history of loyalty programs shows that loyalty currencies are actually swapped out on a regular basis.

Egyptologists have uncovered evidence that ancient Egyptians practised a type of reward program similar to modern frequent flyer programs, including status tiers and the ability to redeem on a wider variety of rewards.

In *Ancient Egypt: Anatomy of A Civilisation*[4] Professor Barry Kemp reminds us that for much of the pharaoh's thousands of years of rule, they didn't have

---

4 Barry J. Kemp, 'Ancient Egypt: Anatomy of a Civilization, 2nd Edition'. 2005

money. It simply wasn't invented yet. Instead, they used a system quite similar to a modern loyalty program.

Citizens, conscripted workers and slaves alike were all awarded commodity tokens (similar to loyalty points or miles) for their work and temple time. The most common were beer and bread tokens. The tokens were physical things, made from wood, then plastered over and painted and shaped like a jug of beer or a loaf of bread.

Interestingly, the more senior people in the hierarchy were rewarded with the same tokens but received bonuses. The Rhind Mathematical Papyrus details examples and mathematical equations regarding how higher positions, such as the skipper, crew leader and doorkeeper, received double bread tokens compared to the rest of the crew. This could be construed as a variant of the status tier bonus, where certain members earn bonus points for transactions to reward them for their loyalty and value to the company.

Interestingly, the tokens could also be exchanged for things other than bread and beer. Those high up enough to earn surplus tokens could redeem them on something else, in the same way that frequent flyer members with lots of points can redeem them both on flights and on non-flight rewards such as iPads, KitchenAid mixers and Gucci handbags.

A more modern history of loyalty program currencies can be traced to the 1700s.

In 1793, a US retailer began rewarding customers with copper tokens, which could be used for future purchases, thereby generating repeat visits which is the core focus of loyalty program design. The idea was quickly replicated by other retailers.[5]

The Grand Union Tea Company was formed in 1872 in Pennsylvania. The owners chose to sidestep retailers and sell their product directly to consumers, starting with door to door sales. They began rewarding customers with tickets which could be collected and redeemed for a wide selection of products from the company's *Catalog of Premiums*.[6] As part of the research for this book, I was fortunate enough to acquire the 1903 version of the *Catalog of Premiums*. In addition to listing the full product range and prices (coffee, tea, spices, extracts, baking powder soap and sundries), it lists 17 pages of rewards

---

5 C. T. &. B. Innovator, "The Loyalty Evolution," New York, 2016.
6 Grand Union Tea Company, 'Catalogue Of Premiums,' 1903.

which include an Oak Roman Chair (100 tickets), lace curtains (120 tickets a pair), Ormolu clock (300 tickets) and dinner set Berlin 1903 (440 tickets). Customers could earn one ticket by buying a pound of coffee at 20 cents, two tickets for premium tea at 40 cents and one ticket for a packet of cloves at 10 cents. The catalogue proudly proclaims, 'We advertise by giving presents with our goods, thus SHARING WITH OUR CUSTOMERS the profits of our business. Remember, you pay less for our goods of same quality than at other stores, and get presents in addition.' It's surprisingly similar to a modern-day loyalty program promotional line.

In the 1890s marketers turned to the physical stamp to reward loyal customers. Customers earned stamps when making purchases and were encouraged to stick them into collecting books. The books could then be exchanged for a wide range of rewards. The Sperry & Hutchinson Company came to dominate this type of loyalty currency approach with their S&H Green Stamps, which could be earned from a range of different retailers in an early form of retail partner coalition program. Sperry & Hutchinson sold the stamps to retailers, who used them to reward customers. At one point, they claimed they were distributing three times as many Green Stamps as the US Postal Service was distributing postal stamps.

Every year Sperry & Hutchinson would release a print version of their catalogue *Ideabook Of Distinguished Merchandise*. In researching the scale of S&H Green Stamp's, I managed to acquire their 1966 *70th Anniversary Edition Ideabook Of Distinguished Merchandise*,[7] which provides a fascinating insight into the scale and complexity of their operations when at the height of their popularity. In addition to being able to order rewards via post, members could visit a vast network of redemption centres, where the entire product range was priced in books of tickets. The 185 page catalogue contains over 2,000 products across 59 categories, a similar sized range to some frequent flyer program online stores. In my copy of the catalogue, an industrious young lady has worked her way through the toys' pages, circling the items she desired and writing out the number of books she needs to claim everything on her list. It provides a sense of the process so many households around the world would

---

7 S&H Green Stamps, 'Ideabook Of Distinguished Merchandise 70th Anniversary Edition,' 1966

have followed in deciding what rewards they wanted to aim for, with much discussion and debate ensuing.

The (pre-computer and internet) logistics for claiming a reward were extensive; the member needed to fill books with stamps, choose the reward products, fill out a separate order form for each reward, then send the books and order forms (plus applicable sales taxes) via first class mail to their nearest distribution centre. The overheads running such a massive operation were enormous.

The 1980s marked the beginning of the end for stamps. The recession of the 1970s created hardship for Sperry & Hutchinson as retail partners sought any way they could to cut costs. Around the same time, American Airlines launched the world's first currency based frequent flyer program using a new currency (miles) which corresponded to how many miles a member had flown. Members could earn miles at a set value for free flights allowing them to easily identify what they could redeem their miles for. Brought on by increasing competition with the deregulation of the US airline industry in 1978, the American Airlines AAdvantage program was soon followed by similar plays from United Airlines, TWA and Delta Airlines. Other airlines around the world quickly replicated. In 1987, Southwest Airlines launched a program which awarded points to members for trips flown, irrespective of the number of miles. Qantas Frequent Flyer launched in Australia with points the same year. Soon after the launch of the early programs, hotel and car rental companies began partnering with the airlines and started offering miles (and soon points) as a way to grow their market share of the lucrative business travellers and high value leisure travellers the programs were designed to appeal to, creating a coalition of retail partners.

With the rapid expansion of the frequent flyer coalition models and their new currencies, other retailers soon replicated their approach and points and miles loyalty programs eventually became the dominant loyalty program currency, ending the ninety year reign of stamps.

From Egyptian tokens to copper tokens to tickets to stamps and then to points and miles; loyalty currencies rise and dominate and are then replaced by something more effective. With the rise of cryptocurrencies, can we now expect points and miles to follow in the path of copper tokens, tickets and stamps?

CHAPTER 3

CRYPTOCURRENCY LOYALTY PROGRAM ADVANTAGES AND CHALLENGES

FROM A LOYALTY perspective, the invention of cryptocurrencies are particularly interesting as they provide an alternative to issuing points and miles.

Despite their 30 or more years of dominance, points and miles (and indeed many of their predecessors) have limitations which can restrict their attractiveness to consumers. Analysis indicates that it may be possible for cryptocurrencies (and cryptotokens) to address some of these shortcomings.

Limited utility

Most loyalty programs only allow points and miles to be used within their own ecosystem on flights, upgrades, an online store, retail vouchers or other company specific discounts.

One advantage cryptocurrencies can provide to members is better liquidity. While cryptocurrencies can be earned and redeemed at participating retailers, they can also be transferred to other members. The loyalty program can even be structured to allow members to transfer their cryptocurrencies to a trading exchange and trade for other cryptocurrencies or cryptotokens, and even for fiat currencies such as US dollars or British pounds. It must be caveated that this option to trade may require additional licencing and regulatory adherence in some countries, which is discussed in Chapter 8. It's also important to point out that the advantage of increased liquidity may be an advantage for the member, but work as a disadvantage for the loyalty program. Many loyalty program operators around the world actively prevent members from redeeming outside their ecosystem to ensure the value remains within their business.

Points expiry

Members who aren't regular users of a loyalty program can suffer their points or miles expiring; points may expire within two years of issuance, or if there is zero account activity (for example, if no points are earned or redeemed within an eighteen month period). Major coalition programs use actuaries to deliberately manage the program to maintain a set expiry rate in order to maximise their program profitability.

Cryptotokens avoid this issue; they don't expire. Once again, this is a benefit for the member, but less so for those loyalty program operators who rely on the expiry to minimise their costs.

Systematic devaluation

A major airline loyalty program launched an online store in 2008 which allows members to redeem points for merchandise and gift cards. This included a $100 gift card for a popular department store for 13,500 points. Today, the same $100 gift card costs 16,800 points. The points have been devalued by the airline over time to generate more profit from the program, penalising loyal members.

Cryptocurrencies are a decentralised currency where the value is principally dependent on market forces. The cryptocurrencies are actively traded on a digital exchange, and just like share-trading, the value increases when demand is greater than supply, and visa-versa. The loyalty program operator cannot simply adjust the value to boost profitability, as the control over value lies with the market. This is one of the core differences between points and miles programs and blockchain loyalty programs, and it is both an opportunity and a challenge; a cryptocurrency which increases in value due to an increase in demand will benefit the members of the program greatly, and likely drive greater program engagement, the core ambition of a loyalty program operator. A cryptocurrency which decreases in value, however, will almost certainly lead to disengagement from the program as members see their benefits eroded. In fact, this appears to be the single greatest risk a cryptocurrency loyalty program faces. In Chapter 7, we discuss theories on how the cryptocurrency value can be best supported to achieve this steady incline, and the serious impacts a significant cryptocurrency value decrease may have on member engagement (hint: it's not good).

General disillusion

Market research and loyalty industry analytics suggest members tend to disengage from major loyalty programs because they don't receive enough value to generate brand loyalty. The 2017 Bond Loyalty Report[8] shows just 25 per cent of members are very satisfied with the level of effort needed to earn a reward or benefit, while only 22 per cent of members perceive their experience with the brand as better than that of non-members. The lack of value delivered to members is a major source of disillusion with loyalty programs in general. Cryptocurrencies have the potential to deliver more value than miles and points, specifically in the instance where a member accumulates cryptocurrencies and they increase in value as a result of higher demand. Once again, the reverse applies; if the value of the cryptocurrency plunges, significant disengagement is likely to follow, a core risk of this program design.

Saturation and homogenisation

Society is suffering from a glut of similar loyalty programs, blending into irrelevance for all but the most dedicated shopper. To stand out from the noise and generate significant hype and consumer interest, blockchain loyalty provides the opportunity for early movers to deliver a differentiated approach to loyalty program design, helping them positively contrast themselves against their competitors. A loyalty currency which is liquid, changes in value and never expires presents a sharp contrast to the points and miles programs of today, providing some valuable material for a marketing team to create campaigns which generate brand cut-through.

---

8 Bond Brand Loyalty, 'The Battle For Love & Loyalty: The Loyalty Report 2017.'

Marketing assault

For years, consumers have suffered from the consistently poor member experience of signing up to a loyalty program only to be bombarded with emails promoting products they don't want. It's a classic ambush play which does significant damage to the loyalty industry as a whole. As a loyalty management consultant, I've studied programs which send up to five emails a week to their members and suffer very high unsubscribe rates as a result, yet still they persist. Through the new field of *blockchain marketing*, members are provided with full control over their data with a secure, blockchain-hosted data wallet for which they hold the private key. They're encouraged to share their personal data in exchange for cryptotoken rewards and are then provided with further rewards if they choose to receive promotional offers from their preferred brands. This revolutionary approach, which hands control of personal data back to the member, has the potential to reinvent marketing on a global scale and nowhere is it better suited than within the core design of a loyalty program. An overview of blockchain marketing is provided in Chapter 15.

As with any innovation some retailers and loyalty program operators will have reservations about utilising cryptotokens as part of a new program design. The three main reservations relate to the stigma attached to cryptocurrency usage, cryptotoken price fluctuations and the adjustment required to the marketing approach:

Cryptocurrency stigmas

In late 2017, I presented the concept of a cryptocurrency loyalty program to a major wholesale company via a loyalty workshop. They wanted a cutting edge loyalty program to generate a direct relationship with their customers who bought their products via a network of retail partners. The CEO was aghast when a cryptocurrency program concept was put forward for consideration. He made it clear he considered Bitcoin (a general label he used for the many different cryptocurrencies and cryptotokens in circulation) to be something that was used by criminal organisations for laundering money and selling drugs and insisted he wanted no involvement with it.

Other loyalty program designers have reported similar strong reactions from their clients. It cannot be ignored that the ignoble roots of early Bitcoin use on drug-trading sites such as Silk Road has generated a notoriety which has tainted the perception of cryptocurrencies. More recently, large amounts of fraud have been committed via ICOs and crypto-related Ponzi schemes. It is something which needs to be addressed directly as part of any serious conversation regarding a blockchain loyalty program. The conversation starts with informing the client that any cryptocurrency loyalty program which allows the member to transfer the cryptotoken out of the program requires the member to pass stringent Anti-Money Laundering (AML) and Counter-Terrorism Funding (CTF) background checks. Thus, it is achievable to build the required regulatory processes into the loyalty program processes to ensure full compliance with global and local legislation.

Wild price fluctuations

It cannot be denied; cryptocurrencies and cryptokens are speculative assets traded on 24 hour exchanges and show a history of fluctuating wildly in price and generating speculative bubbles.

Since the release of the 1st Edition of *Blockchain Loyalty* in 2018, the world has seen a persistent and sustained bear market which has led to many cryptocurrencies and cryptotokens losing over 98% of their value. This includes a number of loyalty program cryptotokens, providing us with the opportunity to determine the impact of significant value reductions on member engagement.

Discussions with major loyalty program operators indicate price fluctuations appear to be the core reason why cryptocurrencies are unlikely to replace points and miles *en masse* anytime soon. While a loyalty currency which can increase in value over time will be naturally attractive, most senior loyalty managers interviewed indicated stability of value is important also, particularly when the member is saving for a higher-value reward. One senior loyalty manager for a major frequent flyer program said that members saving points for an international flight would be devastated if they nearly reached their goal, only for the value of the loyalty currency to drop. 'The backlash,' he said, 'would be very damaging to the brand.'

As a response to this, some blockchain loyalty program operators are focusing on cryptotokens which have static value. A single platform can support hundreds of different retailer programs, with each retailer rewarding their members with a unique, branded cryptotoken. The advantage is interchangeability; a member can redeem their cryptotokens with their preferred retailer, but they also have the option to redeem with any of the other retailers in the network. This approach is detailed in Chapter 6.

Marketing approach

Thanks to consumer use of heuristics (mental shortcuts that ease the cognitive load of making a decision), loyalty programs are able to make the value they provide through points and miles programs sound much bigger than it is. If a member spends $100 with a retailer and that retailer rewards them with 1% of the total spend, then the member will receive $1 of value back. It isn't much and doesn't sound like much. But if it's part of a loyalty program, the member can earn one hundred points (at 1c per point equal to $1). Wow, one hundred points sounds like a lot more than $1! Loyalty programs often run competitions where members can win one million points or miles. That sounds huge, but it is simply loyalty programs exploiting size heuristics, where consumers assume a 'lot' of something equates to 'big'. In reality, the prize value for one million points is generally around $8,000 or less. Thus, using points and miles is an effective way for loyalty programs to promote lots of value without actually delivering lots of value.

The challenge with a blockchain loyalty program is the value of the cryptocurrency is constantly changing, meaning the marketing team can't exploit size heuristics. One hundred cryptotokens may be worth $1 today, but they may be worth $3 tomorrow or even 50c. The loyalty program can't promote a set amount of cryptotokens earned per dollar spent as it may expose them to a higher cost when the member earns. An alternative is to promote a percentage return (for example, receive 1% back in cryptotokens for every dollar spent) but most loyalty marketers interviewed see this position as sub-optimal to promoting the earning of large amounts of points and miles. Suffice to say, blockchain loyalty is still in its infancy, and over the next few years it will be interesting to observe the different ways those pioneer companies position their program offering.

Tax and legal

With cryptocurrencies falling into the area of digital currencies, numerous tax and legal regulations must be complied with. As cryptocurrencies can be traded globally (unlike points and miles) this extends to any country where the program operates, making it a potentially challenging area for a loyalty program operator. Fortunately, most governments have accepted cryptocurrencies aren't going away. While a minority of governments have banned them outright, most governments are busy forming new regulations which allow this new and important technology to evolve. Even more encouragingly, from a loyalty perspective many countries already have tax and legal regulations which a blockchain loyalty program can operate under, and which allow dispensations not available to other blockchain companies. This area is covered more extensively in Chapter 8.

There have been a number of early mover major brands who've successfully made blockchain loyalty plays simply by capitalising on the hype.

Burger King Russia made global headlines when it launched WhopperCoin in August 2017. With each purchase of the burger chain's signature Whopper burger, customers received WhopperCoins which they could exchange for a free burger or transfer to other members. Running on the Waves blockchain platform, one billion WhopperCoins were created and distributed at the rate of one Whoppercoin per ruble spent.

'Now Whopper is not only [a] burger that people in 90 different countries love – it's an investment tool as well,' Ivan Shestov, head of external communications at Burger King Russia was quoted as saying. 'According to the forecasts, cryptocurrency will increase exponentially in value. Eating Whoppers now is a strategy for financial prosperity tomorrow.'[9]

Hooters is famous for one thing, but the launch of their own blockchain loyalty program in January 2018 generated significant interest in their new cryptocurrency, Mobivity Merit tokens. The announcement of the new program was enough to send their share price up 41 per cent. 'Eating a burger is now a way to mine for cryptocoins!' the company proclaimed in a press

---

9 https://www.rappler.com/technology/
news/180456-burger-king-whoppercoin-cryptocurrency-russia

release.[10] The company also announced plans to expand the program to other brands including American Burger Company, BGR, Little Big Burger and Just Fresh.

Kodak also enjoyed a share price increase when it announced the launch of KODAKCoin in January 2018, with the value rising 60 per cent. The KODAKOne platform delivers an encrypted, digital ledger of rights ownership for photographers to register new work as well as archive work that they can then license within the platform. With KODAKCoin, photographers can receive payment for licensing their work immediately upon sale and, for both professional and amateur photographers, sell their work on a secure blockchain platform. The KODAKOne platform is designed to continually crawl websites in order to monitor and protect the intellectual property (IP) of the images registered in the KODAKOne system. Where unlicensed usage of images is detected, the KODAKOne platform can efficiently manage the post-licensing process in order to reward photographers.

'Engaging with a new platform, it is critical photographers know their work and their income is handled securely and with trust, which is exactly what we did with KODAKCoin,' said WENN Digital CEO Jan Denecke. 'Subject to the highest standards of compliance, KODAKCoin is all about paying photographers fairly and giving them an opportunity to get in on the ground floor of a new economy tailored for them, with secure asset rights management built right in.'[11]

What is interesting here is the mix of different approaches. WhopperCoin and Hooters' Mobivity Merit tokens played beautifully as promotional gimmicks, generating big headlines and even bigger share price spikes, much to the companies' credit.

The Kodak approach, however, is something much more profound. It delivers a neat solution using the best feature of blockchain, trust, to solve the real world problem of photographers having their photos used but not receiving any royalties. As with any other society-changing innovation, the gimmicks quickly give way to the practical applications which over time lead to mass adoption.

---

10 http://fortune.com/2018/01/02/hooters-bitcoin-blockchain-cryptocurrency/
11 https://www.kodak.com/corp/press_center/kodak_and_wenn_digital_partner_to_launch_major_blockchain_initiative_and_cryptocurrency/default.htm

CHAPTER 4
LOYALTY 101

As DISCUSSED IN our historical review of loyalty currencies, one of the main opportunities to utilise blockchain within a loyalty program is to swap out points and miles for a cryptocurrency, but keep all the other loyalty program structures which have stood the test of time in place. This can occur while maintaining all the other infrastructure and design elements which support a quality loyalty program. To explore what is required to execute this type of a program at an optimal level, it is critical to dive deeper into pure loyalty program design. What is it that makes a world class loyalty program and can cryptocurrencies fit within this proven framework?

Loyalty programs can be big and small. And some of them are really big! While all of these programs started off with the primary aim of generating increased customer loyalty, they have morphed into massive profit engines. The major coalition loyalty programs such as AAdvantage, Delta SkyMiles, Qantas Frequent Flyer, Nectar, Payback and others generate billions of dollars of revenue each year and measure their profits in the hundreds of millions of dollars.

At the other end of the scale are small programs and my personal favourite loyalty program design; the humble coffee card.

The coffee card is the most successful loyalty program design of all time when based on the number of individual companies who have adopted it. When you explore the elegance of the design, it's not surprising. It's simple to join; simply pick up a card when you buy your coffee and you're a member. It's simple to understand; grab a card, get a stamp for each coffee and earn ten stamps to claim a reward. It's easy to track progress towards the reward; six stamps, four more to go. The reward is perfectly tailored to the desires of the member, which is ultimately free coffee. It's cheap and easy to implement; simply design some paper cards sporting the café's logo and print them.

While all of that is impressive, it's the commercial model underpinning the coffee card design which is the true genius. Think about this scenario; a café wants to sell more coffee, so they consider offering a 10 per cent discount. The only problem is, they have a mix of loyal customers and one off customers, and the latter aren't as price sensitive. Rather than applying the discount, they introduce a coffee card. Their loyal customers get to enjoy a 10 per cent cumulative discount (buying ten coffees and getting one free costs roughly the same as a 10 per cent discount on each of 11 cups) but the one off and irregular customers still pay full price.

Irrespective of whether a loyalty program is big or small, the critical element is member engagement. Numerous studies have shown engaged customers use more products more often, are more satisfied and less likely to switch, are more likely to promote the brand to family and friends and are more open to receiving promotional material.

Member engagement is critical to everything. While it is the ambition of every company to have a large, loyal customer base, for many companies this isn't realistic. A well-designed program can drive deeper engagement right across the board, even from customers who would never see themselves as being loyal to the company. Driving increased engagement from customers inevitably results in some of those customers becoming genuinely loyal, but the company will benefit more from the increased engagement of all their customers, loyal or not. Loyalty manifests from greater engagement. Focus on the engagement and loyalty will arise on its own.

Loyalty benefits are immense. Brand loyal customers declare and demonstrate emotional connections with the brand, continue to purchase over a long period of time and across various product lines, are resistant to discounts and promotions from competitors and often share their positive attitude about the product with others.

Try selling a Samsung phone to an Apple iPhone user (and vice versa) and you'll see the perfect illustration of this phenomena.

Loyalty programs are so prevalent these days that there's a high likelihood that when a customer walks into a retailer or transacts online they'll be asked to join a program.

It is quite common for consumers to join multiple programs over time, fill their wallet or purse up with plastic cards, only to later dispose of the cards belonging to the programs they no longer use, thereby creating space for new loyalty cards. As a result, modern consumers are becoming more considered when deciding whether to join a new program or not. They're also turning to apps such as Stocard, Apple Pay, Samsung Pay and GPay to store their loyalty cards digitally.

I am fanatical about joining new loyalty programs and belong to several hundred programs, mainly because I'm passionate about rigorously studying their mechanisms. I study the join process, onboarding marketing communications, earning value, method for claiming a reward, different engagement elements, retention and win back approaches and most importantly, the treatment I receive as a preferred customer.

Through my years of exploration and investigation, I've identified six core common elements of successful programs. The six elements are: simple, emotional, valuable, surprising, differentiated and developing.

Let's explore each in turn and determine whether a cryptotoken loyalty approach can support or enhance a company's ability to deliver to them.

Simple

A world class loyalty program is simple to join, simple to understand and simple to engage with.

Simple to join

Astoundingly, there are still major retailers who require a new member of their loyalty program to fill in a paper form with excessive amounts of data. Standing at the cashier spending ten minutes filling in a form with a half-chewed ballpoint while busy customers glare and huff waiting to be served is a somewhat awkward and antiquated experience and runs counter to developing a deeper relationship with a brand. And where does that paper form with highly personal information on it end up? As consumers become increasingly security conscious and less willing to share personal data, companies need to consider the information they are asking for and how essential it is.

I once reviewed the join process for a cinema operator. My analysis identified only 55 per cent of new members were completing the registration process, despite the fact they would be rewarded with a free movie ticket. Some of the personal information the cinema was requesting included a mailing address (despite the fact they never mailed anything to their members), work postcode, favourite cinema (despite the fact they could discern this from purchase behaviour) and whether the member was the main grocery shopper in their household. My recommendation involved cutting down the registration process to capture the member's name, email address, password and birthday (so they could send them a present). Not surprisingly, registration completion rates soared. The lesson: while it is tempting to ask for large amounts of information as part of the registration process, companies should identify what information is actually needed (e.g. does the program really need the members mailing address?) or can be accessed post registration (e.g. transaction data denoting preferred products). Ultimately, information should primarily be captured to enhance the member's experience with the brand as a pathway to driving deeper engagement.

From a blockchain loyalty perspective, the recommendation is to provide the member with as many ways to join the program as possible, which also allows them to continue to engage in the way that suits them best. This includes physical and digital membership cards, biometric scans, apps, credit and debit cards, stored value cards and other options. We cover these in detail in Chapter 13.

Simple to understand

As the program increases in complexity, the challenge is keeping it simple enough for members to make sense of it. A coffee drinker joining a coffee card program can understand very quickly how the program works; buy a coffee, earn a stamp; buy 10 coffees, get a free coffee. Whereas, frequent flyer programs are incredibly complex; members earn points across hundreds of partners and redeem points on flights, upgrades, lounge access, gift cards and consumer goods and even at partner stores. While a program should be simple to join, understand and engage with, that doesn't mean it can't be complex in design. It just requires educating the customer on the mechanisms via the join and onboarding process. Additionally, hundreds of earn partners can be condensed into a small number of categories, rather than thousands of reward options. The program recommends particular options which the member may be able to achieve in a reasonable timeframe based on their earn trajectory.

Blockchain loyalty programs may seem complex— members earn a cryptocurrency which fluctuates in value due to trading activity on digital exchanges— but it's not always the case.

The first step to make the program understandable is to fit it into a framework that the member will recognise; they shop, earn cryptocurrency and redeem the cryptocurrency for rewards or sell them on an exchange.

The second step is to focus on the core difference between other programs and the blockchain loyalty program and sell it as an attractive, fun benefit; unlike other programs where the points value stays static, the cryptocurrency value can go up or down, just like a game.

Some blockchain loyalty companies are providing cryptotokens which remain static in value to make it even simpler for members to understand, which is covered in Chapter 6.

Simple to engage with

I once joined a program for Huggies nappies. The program concept *seemed* simple; buy Huggies products, collect virtual stars and redeem for free Fisher Price toys. That was until I bought some Huggies nappies and attempted to engage with the program. To earn virtual stars, the following steps were required:

Purchase any Huggies nappies, nappy-pants and baby wipes products listed.

Log onto the promotion website and click on the "claim stars" link.

Accurately enter the following details, including the date of purchase, quantities and barcode of the eligible product plus the store of purchase and receipt number.

And it didn't end there. I was required to upload a photo/electronic copy of the receipts that clearly displayed the store and purchase details. And then I was required to log in/sign up to a loyalty account.

Finally, an option to click 'claim' became available, but by then they had already lost me.

A loyalty program is primarily designed to drive deeper member engagement, so making it difficult to engage with is irony at its best. In this age of highly advanced technology and innovation, offering a program which involves any level of complexity in accessing the benefits is unforgivable. It is lazy thinking and execution and has no place in a modern consumer environment where the customer must be at the centre of everything.

For blockchain loyalty programs, this means utilising the latest technology to make it easy to earn and redeem. The identification and redemption process must be woven into the structure of the transaction, so it requires little effort from the customer and spending cryptocurrencies should be no harder than spending cash.

Emotional

The ultimate ambition and essential foundation of any loyalty program is to develop an emotional connection between the member and the brand. Loyal members that have emotional connections with the brand will continue to purchase over a long period of time and across various product lines. These members are resistant to discounts and promotions from competitors and often share their positive attitude about the product with others.

The best way to tackle the challenge of garnering brand loyalty is with outstanding program design. While loyalty to a brand is greater than just the loyalty program, it provides the company with the opportunity to understand the member as an individual and provide tailored service and experiences.

Naked Wines is a great example of a company going to the extreme to deliver unique and personalised experiences at scale. The central tenet of Naked Wines proposition is the Angel member. Angels help a network of smaller, talented winemakers to make wines by providing them with guaranteed sales via a distribution channel that delivers a reasonable margin. Angels support the winemakers by depositing as little as A$40 per month into their Naked Wines account towards their next order. The money can be spent on any wine whenever the Angel wants. In return, Angels save at least 25 per cent on each order. Naked Wines encourage their Angels to download their app, which automatically loads the member's order history. This makes it easy and fun for Angels to rate and review the wines they've tasted and feel part of an exclusive community.

As part of my loyalty research, I purchased a number of cases from Naked Wines, drank all of it and wrote some reviews. A few days after submitting my reviews, I received personal responses from each of the winemakers, thanking me for my feedback; a personal touch which made me feel much closer to the brand. A few weeks later I celebrated my birthday and I was delighted to receive an email from Naked Wines complete with a link to a video of one of the winemakers singing *Happy Birthday*. But it wasn't just any winemaker. It was Jen Pfeiffer, the creator of Diamond Label Shiraz 2015, a wine I had rated very highly. In addition, Naked Wines offered me a free bottle of The Diamond Durif 2015 as a present, another of Jen Pfeiffer's magnificent creations. This brilliantly personalised package left me feeling emotionally connected to the Naked Wines brand and to a creator of one of their products which further fostered my loyalty and willingness to continue to spend with them.

Taking it a step further, psychology shows us that consumers don't just feel emotional connections to preferred brands but they actually adopt them as part of their identity. In 1978, Henry Tajfel proposed social identity theory[12]. Social identity is a person's sense of who they are based on their membership of different groups. Tajfel theorised that groups which people belonged to as social classes (such as sporting teams, families, groups of friends, workplaces etc) were an important source of pride and self-esteem. Groups give us a sense of social identity and a sense of belonging to the social world.

This theory found further support when Schwarz, Strack, Kommer & Wagner[13] found football fans who followed a winning team reported higher levels of life satisfaction than those whose team was consistently losing. Football fans take on their team as part of their own identity, so much so that

---

12 Tajfel, H. & Turner, J. C., 'An Integrative Theory of Intergroup Conflict', 1979
13 Schwarz, N., Strack, F., Kommer, D. & Wagner, D., 'Soccer, rooms, and the quality of your life: Mood effects on judgments of satisfaction with life in general and with specific domains', 1987

the team's performance has a pronounced psychological impact on the perspective they have on their own life.

Bhattacharya and Sen[14] took this further by exploring social identity theory as it related to brands. They proposed that 'strong consumer-company relationships often result from consumers identification with those companies, which helps them satisfy one or more important self-definitional needs'. In other words, consumers connect with brands in much the same way they connect with their social class, sporting teams and friendship groups and the brand plays a critical role in making them feel better about themselves by increasing their self-esteem.

For the modern loyalty program designer, this insight is highly profound; a program which serves to make the member feel a sense of exclusivity and belonging will play a central role in the member adopting the brand (sub consciously or otherwise) as an element of their own self-definition. Think of a Platinum Frequent Flyer boarding the plane first and feeling good about themselves because of what they belong to and the exclusive privileges they enjoy.

The opportunities here for blockchain loyalty programs are vast. Cryptocurrencies have the potential to increase in value when the number of retailers and members grow, which makes the whole program community-centric. This is because the number of cryptocurrency units available is limited, whereas the number of retailers and members who can participate isn't. By building and having the community come together to focus more of their spend on participating retailers, the value of the cryptocurrency can go up, benefiting everyone.

Analysis of cryptocurrency traders on social media sites such as Twitter, Reddit, Telegram and Slack show almost cult like followings of blockchain companies and cryptocurrencies. While there are many online forums supporting discussions relating to different loyalty points and miles programs, these primarily relate to strategies for maximising earn and complaints about program changes. In contrast, leaders of blockchain companies are perceived as something akin to Gods by members of their communities. A great example is Justin Sun, founder of Tron, who is portrayed by his fans in memes as a Messiah and a Chinese general.

---

14 Bhattacharya, C.B. and Sen, S., 'Consumer-Company Identification: A Framework for Understanding Consumers' Relationships with Companies', 2003

Valuable

Of the six principles, *valuable* is arguably the most important. A member will join a program because of the promise of value. And the same member will continue to engage with the program if they perceive they are gaining value from doing so. The world is full of loyalty programs with large member bases of which a significant proportion are partially or fully disengaged as a result of the member no longer believing there is any value to be extracted. The card ends up in the bin, the app is deleted and the member unsubscribes from all marketing communications. A disengaged member is the worst possible outcome for a brand, even worse than a non-member. At least with a non-member there is a chance to encourage them to join and use that opportunity to drive a closer relationship. It is very difficult to win back a member who has disengaged because of a lack of perceived value as their mind is already made up and their decision based on direct experience.

A major frequent flyer program signed up a market leading supermarket chain as an earn partner. The multimillion dollar marketing campaign was populated with images of international travel destinations such as the Eiffel Tower, the Statue Of Liberty, Big Ben and an iPad in a shopping basket. New member expectations were set that if they shopped at that supermarket they would soon be flying all around the world. The campaign was hugely success-ful in driving new member subscriptions, with many millions of consumers taking up the program's loyalty card to swipe at the supermarket.

Within 12 months, however, a significant proportion of the new members had either stopped swiping their cards altogether or showed advanced signs of reducing their swipe behaviour. Both the frequent flyer program and the supermarket were shocked. How was it that a program partnership which had launched with such success could have such a large disengagement rate?

Analysis quickly identified the issue. The supermarket partnership had attracted two types of member groups; those who already belonged to the frequent flyer program and were interested to access a new earn channel and those who joined the frequent flyer program because of the supermar-ket partnership.

The first group showed ongoing high levels of swipe behaviour and even demonstrated an increase in basket size over time; a great success for the super-market. The second group proved problematic. Members who joined the frequent flyer program because of the supermarket partnership only seemed to be earning points in one channel; the supermarket. And because their average weekly spend was quite low, the number of points they earnt was low and very short of the points needed to fly to see the Eiffel Tower, the Statue of Liberty and Big Ben or get a new iPad. In fact, most of those members didn't even have enough points to access a $20 gift card. The launch marketing campaign had promised massive value and members had joined with the expectation they would be able to access that value. But over time, week after week, dutifully swiping their card, they realised they weren't progressing towards their goal.

These are the conditions by which disengagement with a loyalty program is most likely to take place and once it manifests, it's very hard to win the member back. The frequent flyer programs' strategic response was to run marketing campaigns targeting the disengaged members to educate them about other channels where they could earn points. It was relatively successful for a proportion of the base, particularly in stimulating some of these members to start flying. But for most of the disengaged members it was too late. Cards in the bin, app deleted and marketing unsubscribed.

For a company looking to deliver value to members through its loyalty program, cryptocurrencies provide a possible solution. A loyalty currency which can increase in value as the popularity of the program grows provides a wonderful incentive for members to continue engaging with the program, even if the amount they're earning for each transaction is low. It is the future potential value which members will be inspired by.

In 1947, Bruner and Goodman[15] conducted an experiment where they asked children to estimate the size of different coins. What they identified was that the poorer the household the child came from, the larger they estimated the coin size to be. It was the fantasy of having a coin which made it seem larger than it was in the imaginations of these children. While it might be a stretch to draw direct parallels between disadvantaged children in postwar Britain and modern loyalty program members, the same effect can be seen to persist; a member earning a cryptotoken which can increase in value is likely to overestimate the amount it is worth because of the fantasy of its

---

15 Bruner, J.S. and Goodman, C.C., 'Value and Need as Organizing Factors in Perception', 1947

future potential. Thus, a member is likely to value $10 of cryptocurrency more highly than $10 of static points or miles.

Of course, the reverse is also true. If a loyalty cryptotoken plummets in value, the loyalty program will almost certainly suffer wide-spread member disengagement, particularly if members with large account holdings don't feel confident the value will rebound. This is one of the key risks for blockchain loyalty programs, and the persistent bear market which began in early 2018 has provided us with a number of case studies which demonstrate the negative impact of a significant value drop. Interestingly, members who don't have large cryptotoken balances (such as those who have recently redeemed their account balance or recently joined the program) aren't negatively impacted by a cryptotoken value reduction but actually benefit, as they'll earn more of the cryptotoken for each transaction they make. This whole area of price fluctuations and the impacts is covered extensively in Chapter 7.

Surprising

As a technique for driving deeper member engagement, surprise and delight is incredibly powerful from a consumer psychology perspective. Several psychological studies suggest that when a customer's expectations are met they will be satisfied and when a customer's expectations are exceeded they will be slightly more satisfied but when a customer is surprised and delighted their satisfaction levels will be off the charts. Let's explore why this is the case.

In 1987, psychologist Norbert Schwarz[16] ran a study (which has parallels to Schwarz, Strack, Kommer & Wagner's research) to test the power of something positive happening on a subject's overall life satisfaction. He placed a small coin on a photocopier for the next user to find. He then conducted an interview with those who found the small coin about their life perspective. 'Those who found the coin were more happy and more satisfied and wanted to change their lives less than those who didn't find a coin,' reported Schwarz. The value is irrelevant; it's significant that something positive and surprising happened to them. Making someone's day and changing their perspective can incur relatively little cost.

A decade later, Mellers, Schwartz, Ho and Ritov[17] further explored the

16 Schwartz, N., 'Stimmung als Information (Mood as information)', 1987
17 Mellers, B.A., Schwartz, A., Ho, K. & Ritov, I., 'Decision Affect Theory:

power of surprise and delight by looking at the difference between expected and unexpected positive outcomes. Their decision affect theory demonstrated that unexpected outcomes have a greater emotional impact than expected outcomes, even when the reward was of lower value. Smaller, surprising wins were shown to be more elating than larger, expected wins. In one experiment the researchers used simple gambling games to test their hypothesis and found a surprise $5 win was rated as more enjoyable by subjects than an expected $9 win.

In the same year, Oliver, Rust & Varki[18] developed a customer delight model which hypothesised the loyalty psychology underpinning this effect. They found evidence to support the notion that positive surprise and delight experiences elicit pleasure, joy and elation and lead to an increase in customer loyalty. They also proved that delight is a positively valenced state reflecting high levels of consumption-based affect and the experience of delight creates a desire for future recurrences of the sensation via the repetition of consumption, which creates loyalty.

The important learning here is the power of surprise and delight. While many companies focus large amounts of effort and cost on points or discount programs, they often neglect to take the opportunity to seed the member's experience with small, low-cost delights. As the research shows, if executed well these can be significantly more powerful in generating loyalty than large points balances.

There is evidence to suggest surprise and delight activity can also improve a customer's liking towards a brand. Regan from Cornell University[19] ran a study where a participant provided an unexpected bottle of Coca-Cola to the subject. Subjects reported liking the person giving the free Coke more than when no Coke was provided. Furthermore, subjects felt more obliged to return a favour to the participant (in this case buy some raffle tickets) when they had accepted the drink (categorised as the reciprocity effect). This highlights another benefit of surprise and delight approaches— if a member receives an

Emotional Reactions to the Outcomes of Risky Options', 1997

18 Oliver, R.L., Rust, R. & Varki, S., 'Customer Delight: Foundations, Findings, and Managerial Insight,' 1997

19 Regan, R., 'Effects of a favor and liking on compliance,' 1971

unexpected benefit from a company, they may feel an obligation to transact with the company to reciprocate; a deeply ingrained psychological drive.

Most importantly, delighted customers have been shown to demonstrate higher loyalty to a company. Berman[20] reported significantly higher levels of loyalty from delighted versus satisfied customers. 'Other potential positive consequences of delight include lower costs due to increased word-of-mouth promotion, lower selling and advertising costs, lower customer acquisition costs, higher revenues due to higher initial and repeat sales, and long-term strategic advantages due to increased brand equity and increased ability to withstand new entrants.' Berman cites one study where 'Mercedes-Benz USA found that the likelihood that a client who is dissatisfied with the service at a retailer will buy or lease from the same retailer is only 10 percent. Mere satisfaction produces a 29 percent likelihood of rebuy or re-lease. However, the likelihood of a delighted client rebuying or re-leasing is 86 percent.'

With all this evidence, it is important that a surprise and delight strategy is considered as a core component of the overall loyalty program. For blockchain loyalty programs, the opportunity is already woven into the program design; it is the cryptocurrency itself. The fact that the currency value can fluctuate quite wildly will provide ample surprise moments and every time it increases in value the member will be truly delighted. Once again, this is a double-edge sword; a negative surprise, such as a significant value decrease, can deliver the opposite of delight and will act to drive disengagement.

Another opportunity for blockchain loyalty program operators is to deliver an Airdrop. This is where members are provided with free cryptotokens to thank them for being part of the program. While the currency has a value, it has been created by the program operator for little cost to them, so they have the ability to draw on their reserves at strategic times to reward their members with a campaign which will certainly generate a loyal following. Airdrops have been seen to generate significant anticipation amongst cryptocurrency holders and from a loyalty perspective they can also be used to motivate members to follow specific behaviours, such as shopping at certain retailers or buying certain brands.

---

20 Berman, B., 'How to delight your customers,' 2005

Differentiated

Having studied hundreds of different loyalty programs across many industries, I have identified that the biggest challenge the loyalty industry faces is too many programs of a similar design, leading to a state of loyalty fatigue, particularly amongst younger demographics. I have viewed multiple qualitative market research sessions where the participants have reported joining a few programs, not receiving any value and not just discarding the program but giving up on loyalty programs entirely in dismay!

Another phenomenon is the tendency for different companies in the same industry to mimic each other's loyalty approaches so they all end up with a very similar program design, despite the fact there are countless effective designs to choose from. Consider the similarities amongst loyalty programs within the hotel or car rental industries.

Numerous text books and articles state the importance of product and service differentiation to gain a competitive advantage, however an often overlooked opportunity is differentiation in loyalty program design. In particular, a differentiated loyalty program provides an occasion to facilitate a discussion with members (which isn't just about price) and positively contribute to the value equation in a way that conventional discounting can't do.

In an industry where everyone rushes to the same space, the opportunity arises for a competitor to gain market share by doing something completely different.

Once again, blockchain loyalty programs deliver to this principle. A loyalty cryptocurrency is something the world has never seen before and as covered in Chapter 3, it delivers a range of benefits compared to points and miles. Companies which announced blockchain loyalty programs, such as Hooters and Kodak, saw significant valuation increases in their shares. A company looking to quickly differentiate themselves from their competitors in a homogenised market could do worse than consider a cryptotoken loyalty program.

Developing

One of the mistakes I often witness with companies across different industries is the tendency to design a loyalty program, implement it and then never change it. It is a classic 'do it big, but do it once,' approach which ignores the modern principles of focussing on the customer.

The strategic advice I provide to my clients is to launch a framework model, which contains elements that can be swapped in and out depending on how members respond to them. Once they have established useable analytics and implemented a member feedback loop they can evolve the program over time. Thus, companies can launch a framework and in one to two years allow it to develop into an effective program, guided by member insight and interaction.

It surprises me how few companies are comfortable with the idea of running short test and learn trials on different iterative product or loyalty program development ideas. The advantages of such an approach are numerous; it is easier to draw conclusions using live experiments than by studying historical or market research data. It is an approach anyone can quickly master and, if successful, the enhancements can quickly expand to the entire customer base.

This is particularly important for a modern approach such as blockchain loyalty programs. The program operations team need to ensure optimisation of the different ways members can engage with the program (for example, is the app design concise and easy to navigate?) and that the general understanding of how the program works is comprehensible ('what do you mean the value of my points can go up or down?'). Because blockchain loyalty is a very new phenomenon, the clear rules of how to execute are only now being devised. It is very similar to the situation facing early website designers who applied test and learn strategies to determine better homepage design and navigation approaches.

Blockchain loyalty doesn't necessarily make delivery of this principle easier but an ever-developing program must be embraced to ensure the execution is successful.

CHAPTER 5
BLOCKCHAIN LOYALTY RESEARCH

IN EARLY 2017, I spent some time searching for good quality empirical blockchain loyalty research. Several blockchain loyalty companies had already launched, with some of them running successful ICOs generating millions of dollars of investment. I naively assumed there were research projects to support the visions stated in their whitepapers. I found nothing.

Inspired by the complete absence of genuine research, I partnered with two other loyalty companies and the University of NSW (UNSW) School of Computer Science and Engineering to run the world's first blockchain loyalty research project. The two companies were PiCoLabs and Loyalty Corp.

PiCoLabs (*www.picolabs.co*) developed the PiCo RetailCloud which helps physical retail stores compete better with pure play online retailers who use modern cloud based data marketing tools to drive customer engagement. Most point of sale (POS) systems in mid-market and enterprise retail chains are proprietary and outdated. This restricts the ability of retail marketers to deliver anything more than rudimentary promotions and customer reward programs in store. With little budget to upgrade, most great marketing initiatives fail to execute due to the limitation of legacy POS. PiCoLabs solved this widespread global problem by developing a plug and play hardware solution which connects any POS to the RetailCloud to enable capture of member ID, real-time earn and redemption, discounts, digital voucher usage and capture of receipt data.

Loyalty Corp (*www.loyaltycorp.com.au*) is a full service agency with an expert team that delivers end to end solutions for some of the world's largest organisations. Loyalty Corp are accredited as a Level 1 PCI-DSS and ISO 27001 and 9001 company, indicative of their commitment and mission to revolutionise the loyalty and payments space globally. Loyalty Corp provide services across design, marketing, platform, payments, integration, product development, reward supply, customer service and account management.

We were fortunate enough to receive support for the project from Professor Salil S. Kanhere and Professor Ron Van der Meyden from the School of Computer Science and Engineering, plus Senior Lecturer Eric Lim from the School of Information Systems and Technology Management, to design the project, recruit members and conduct the analysis (refer to the Appendix for the official research paper). We also received some expert advice from Daniel Bar of *bitfwd*.

To run the research, we created a live market loyalty program called *Unify Rewards* which mimicked other loyalty programs, with the main difference being the reward currency issued was a popular cryptocurrency: Ether. The trial ran from 1 October to 18 November 2017.

Twelve retailers at UNSW, Sydney, were enrolled as program retailers. To earn Ether, participants conducted a transaction at any of the retailers. They were permitted to earn up to $10 of Ether every two days. They were not required to create a separate Ether digital wallet, as their balance was held for them in trust. This proved to be significant in simplifying engagement with the program, as many of the members didn't have an Ether wallet and didn't understand how to create one.

Participants had a range of options for redeeming their Ether balance. Throughout the trial they could:

- Cash their balance into an eWallet. The Ether was sold at the actual market rate and the fiat currency was transferred into an eWallet held within the web app. They could use the balance to access a discount on a range of popular gift cards.

- Cash their balance into a bank account. The Ether was sold at the actual market rate and the fiat currency was transferred into the participants' nominated bank account.

- Transfer their balance to another participant, simply by using the recipient's registered email address.

At the end of the trial, participants were also provided with the opportunity to transfer their balance to their personal Ether wallet. For those participants who didn't have one, instructions and support were provided on how to create one.

The earn of Ether during the trial was weighted towards high engagement:

- 21 per cent of participants didn't transact at all (registered but didn't engage further).

- 18 per cent transacted but not enough to earn Ether.

- 61 per cent earned at least $10 of Ether (achieving the research project target for engagement as it allowed them to earn at least one allocation of Ether).

- Even more encouragingly, 18 per cent of members earned $20 or more of Ether.

This is a very high engagement rate for a loyalty program compared to industry averages. By comparison, two major loyalty programs in Australia show member engagement rates of 57 per cent (a major supermarket chain) and 37 per cent (a major liquor chain).

Engagement with the marketing communications was consistently high. The minimum open rate for email communications was 48.3 per cent and the maximum was 72.7 per cent, well above the industry average for loyalty programs which can be as low as 11 per cent[21].

With respect to redemption behaviour:

- 67 per cent of participants chose to transfer their Ether to their personal Ether wallet.

- 29 per cent of participants chose to cash in their Ether for a deposit into their bank account.

- 4 per cent of participants chose to cash in their Ether to use for a gift card.

- 0 per cent of participants transferred their Ether allocation to another participant.

The outcome indicated a strong propensity from a majority of participants to hold their Ether for speculative purposes, an advantage cryptocurrencies

21 Smart Insights, "Email marketing engagement and response statistics 2018.'

and tokens have over loyalty points and one which the survey results identified as being particularly attractive to members.

Results from the post pilot survey indicated participants were generally well exposed to points based loyalty programs, with only one respondent indicating they didn't belong to any program. This confirmed participants had sufficient insight to compare a points program to a cryptocurrency program.

Overwhelmingly, the results indicated participants found a cryptocurrency program to be more engaging than a points program.

Respondents reported the following:

- They found Unify Rewards to be more rewarding than their favourite loyalty program (7.58/10 versus 6.04/10).

- They felt Unify Rewards was more motivating in influencing them to spend their money with participating retailers than their favourite loyalty program (7.80/10 versus 5.98/10).

- They reported both Unify Rewards and their favourite loyalty program had motivated them to modify the way they spent money to maximise their loyalty currency earn (83 per cent for Unify Rewards versus 80 per cent for their favourite loyalty program). This is a strong result for both approaches and provides evidence that loyalty programs can be very effective in influencing consumer spending behaviour.

- They provided a higher Net Promoter Score for Unify Rewards than their favourite loyalty program (8.53/10 versus 5.72/10).

- 59 per cent spent more money on campus during the trial period. A further 41 per cent spent the same.

- 86 per cent felt Unify Rewards was more appealing than their favourite loyalty program and 11 per cent felt it was just as appealing.

Some of the positive reasons cited included:

- 'The concept is interesting since the value can fluctuate.'

- 'There's a bit of mystery about Ether – it's a bit of a wild card so there's an element of speculation and potential that makes it exciting. But it's not a guaranteed thing.'

- 'Cryptocurrency is cool, [the program] exposed me to it.'

- 'Cryptocurrency is a very exciting currency as it fluctuates and you never know what to expect the next day. It might go up or go down and it is a great experience to learn about how it works and what influences it.'

- 'The possibility of growing value and ability to cash out when you like is very attractive.'

- '[It's] more appealing because of the tangible dollar value of the Ether as opposed to less tangible points.'

- 'Ether feels like you're getting money rather than "points". When Ether was low, I was incentivised to spend and reach the next 10 before Ether spiked.'

Some of the negative reasons cited included:

- 'There is too much fluctuation with cryptocurrency.'

- 'It was an interesting reward but also felt to be of little difference to cash.'

Further analysis of the survey data identified evidence to suggest surveyed participants who were less satisfied with the level of reward from existing loyalty schemes were more likely to find earning Ether more appealing.

One critique of the study was that earning a cryptocurrency was really no different than earning cash. While some members drew comparisons with cash, the overwhelming opinion from members indicated they felt cryptocurrencies were more exciting and desirable due to value fluctuations ('you never know what to expect the next day') and the potential for a significant future value increase ('there's an element of speculation and potential that makes it exciting'). It is also telling that 67 per cent of participants chose to hold (or HODL) their Ether rather than cash it in. In that sense, we perceived the cryptocurrency injected a unique and highly engaging gamified element into the program which is absent from points and miles programs, and cash back programs.

In fact, this was the most exciting insight derived from the study. Discussions with some of the participants indicated they became obsessed about the value of Ether and their account balance during the trial and checked the value on average five times a day. Compare this to a points or miles program, where the average member rarely checks their balance because the value of their holding remains constant. It is unlikely someone would even check their bank balance five times a day. Considering the primary purpose of a loyalty program is to drive deeper member engagement, this insight really cemented the enormous potential of blockchain loyalty in the minds of the research team. If a loyalty program can be created with a currency which members obsess over and regularly check the value of, then they're much more likely to be thinking about the program and the brand and how to acquire more. They're also more likely to be accessing the program app, viewing program promotions and talking with others about the program.

Our world first field trial demonstrated cryptocurrencies have the potential to be an effective substitute loyalty currency for points and miles. Although further research is required to explore the potential of cryptocurrencies in future loyalty program design, our research showed that offering Ether as an alternative to points and miles generated very strong engagement, with 86 per cent of survey respondents reporting they found it to be more appealing than the points they earn from their favourite loyalty program.

More widely, it also demonstrated loyalty programs have the potential to play a key role in mainstreaming cryptocurrency ownership and adoption for a few reasons; firstly, setting up an exchange account to buy cryptocurrency is complicated, whereas signing up for a loyalty program is quick and simple, making it much more accessible. Secondly, trading in a highly volatile market such as cryptocurrencies can be incredibly risky, whereas a loyalty program allows members to earn cryptocurrency without them having to risk their own money. Thirdly, at the time of writing it is still very difficult to spend cryptocurrencies in a retail setting. Loyalty programs have the means to deliver digital wallets to be used across a coalition of retail partners to spend cryptocurrency balances, ensuring real world utility (although this wasn't part of the research functionality).

There were some limitations in our research; the Unify Rewards earn approach was simplistic and didn't consider the amount of spend made in each transaction. A new research project which ties the amount of cryptocurrency earned to the amount spent would provide additional insight into whether cryptocurrency loyalty programs are more effective in driving higher transactional spend than points and miles programs.

Another aspect which was not possible to measure with Unify Rewards is the effectiveness of a new cryptotoken in driving engagement. While some companies may choose to utilise existing, popular cryptocurrencies such as Bitcoin and Ether, the bigger commercial opportunity is for a company to create an original cryptotoken with full control over the amount created and how it is distributed. This involves a greater investment to build awareness of (and desire for) the currency and would require a longer timeframe to determine any results.

CHAPTER 6

USING CRYPTOCURRENCIES TO POWER A LOYALTY PROGRAM

THIS CHAPTER WILL cover the four main areas where cryptocurrencies and cryptotokens can be used within loyalty programs:

1. A loyalty program powered by a single new cryptotoken

2. A loyalty program powered by an existing cryptocurrency

3. Many loyalty programs powered by multiple new cryptotokens on a single platform

4. A security token supported by a loyalty program

Let's explore each of these in turn.

1. A loyalty program powered by a single new cryptotoken

To date, this model has been the most prevalent of all blockchain loyalty approaches, although many of the existing program operators have been unsuccessful thus far in realising their strategic ambitions. The approach involves the company creating a finite amount of a new cryptotoken, which they can provide to members as an alternative to points and miles. Because the amount of cryptotokens is finite, if enough demand can be generated (via members earning them through transacting with participating retailers), the value should increase via basic supply and demand economics. The full commercial model explaining how this design works is covered in Chapter 7.

The main challenge is the same one all loyalty program operators have faced since the days of Ancient Egypt; acquiring sufficient numbers of retailers and members to participate in the program. Recruiting retailers and members can be incredibly tough. A coalition loyalty program (where members can earn points across multiple retailers) is a classic chicken and egg business model. Members won't join the program if there are no retailers to earn from. Retailers won't join the program if there are no members to shop at their stores. This is the reason why there are so few successful loyalty coalition programs around the world. And in most circumstances the successful ones have been built off the back of already successful businesses.

Think airlines, who already had large customer bases when they first launched frequent flyer programs. The problem they solved is how to reward loyal customers with spare seats they couldn't sell without devaluing the product through heavy discounting. Creating a points currency allowed them to deliver those heavy discounts to their most loyal customers, but the discount was disguised.

Without it being their primary intention, the airlines created a desirable currency, which they realised they could sell to other companies and generate a new revenue line. The critical point is they didn't start with nothing. Early on they had a significant member base and a way for members to earn reasonable points balances via flying activity. They had what they needed to crank the engine.

For the new blockchain loyalty companies, the question remains; they have their cryptotokens, but how will they engage a core base of retailers and members to convert them into 'desirable' cryptotokens? While this is important for a points and miles loyalty program, is critically important for a blockchain loyalty program, because the demand for the token is what builds the growth and price stability in the cryptotoken's value.

Let's look at some of the players who are operating cryptotoken loyalty programs. This list is by no means exhaustive, with new companies emerging every day which are regularly featured on *www.blockchainloyalty.io*.

CampusCoin

www.campuscoinproject.org

CampusCoin is a university focused blockchain loyalty program and is designed to tap into university communities to act as recruiters for retailers and members.

Students can register to be an ambassador for their university and earn bounties in CampusCoin. This includes daily bonuses for encouraging students to sign up for the CampusCoin app, large bonuses for convincing retailers on campus to start accepting CampusCoin and further rewards for convincing local bars and restaurants to accept CampusCoin. While CampusCoin doesn't provide any information on their website regarding the number of universities or business who provide CampusCoin earn, they have managed to sign up ambassadors across 58 universities worldwide.

One of the key drawbacks of the current CampusCoin process is the complexity of accessing it. Members must buy Bitcoin, then exchange Bitcoin for CampusCoin. Then once a member has it, the only thing they can do with it is redeem it back into Bitcoin and then cash. CampusCoin state on their website that in the future students will be able to redeem CampusCoin at participating retailers but until then it seems to be a currency without a purpose other than day trading.

The biggest challenge they face in gaining traction would appear to be signing up retailers. Convincing a retailer to join a loyalty program is an incredibly difficult task and trying to remotely recruit a group of student ambassadors to perform that task on one's behalf is even more difficult.

CampusCoin launched in mid-2017 with one coin valued at 0.02 cents. By early 2018, CampusCoin was trading at five cents, an increase of 250 times! Those students who purchased CampusCoin early in the program and sold at the peak would likely have been able to cover their college fees with the profits. By early-2018, the price had flat-lined at just 0.0003 cents with almost no volume, making the program look fairly unhealthy. That being said, the website promotes a robust development roadmap, including the ability for individual universities to own a private sub-ledger, and a credit system which protects investors against unexpected value declines.

Incent

www.incentloyalty.com

Incent is an Australian-based blockchain loyalty program described as, 'a reward you can earn instantly for doing the things you love. Watch, shop, or dine and see your rewards grow!'

Members of the program can earn Incent for shopping at 350 online retailers and a small number of retail partners, and for watching e-Sports.

Incent raised A$1m in late 2016. The price started at 9 cents before rocketing to US$1.03 at the height of the 2017-2018 bull market. By early-2019 the price has fallen to 4 cents.

An interview with the founder, Rob Wilson, indicated a solid commitment to the program and a robust development roadmap. A team of developers and designers are working long hours to bring new innovations to life while a business development team works to expand their partner network.

LoyalCoin

www.loyalcoin.io

LoyalCoin is the invention of Appsolutely, a Philippines based loyalty company with a platform which integrates into point of sale systems and offers white label app based solutions.

They have an impressive portfolio of clients, including Petron, Starbucks, Havaianas, Bench, American Eagle Outfitters, TGI Fridays, Aldo and Cotton On, which gives them a firm foundation to push for retailer participation in the new program.

In early 2018, LoyalCoin raised around US$16 million via ICO. They launched on Cryptopia exchange on the 31st May 2018 and traded at $0.0065. By early-2019 the price had reduced to $0.001, but daily trading volume was still reasonably high at around US$1m per day, making them one of the better performing loyalty cryptotokens.

I interviewed Appsolutely's CEO Patrick E. Palacios about the progress of the LoyalCoin program.

He informed me some of the funds raised from the ICO were used to build their LoyalWallet which allows members to earn LoyalCoin and redeem rewards anytime, anywhere. The registration process includes a simple KYC

(Know Your Customer) process, with the member rewarded with a LoyalCoin airdrop for successful completion. Members can earn further LoyalCoin for referring family and friends to join.

As with any coalition loyalty program, the key to success is in the merchant partnerships, and it's here that LoyalCoin is really showing their true strength.

'We've recently launched a major partnership with 7-11 in The Philippines,' Palacios said. 'They were attracted by the social media buzz around LoyalCoin, as well as the obsession by Filipino millennials with cryptocurrencies.' This is in a country where an estimated 80-85% don't have bank accounts, making cryptocurrencies a perfect fit.

Another partnership is with Grab Philippines, the country's version of Uber, to allow riders to pay for rides using LYL tokens. Additional partnerships have been announced with Philippine Airlines, McDonalds, SM (a major shopping mall chain), Petron gas stations and Cebu Pacific.

Appsolutely are negotiating further major partnerships, including a large coffee chain in South Korea comprised of over one hundred stores. Appsolutely have also partnered with a number of payment providers who make it easy for members to redeem LoyalCoin across a wide range of retailers. 'We're targeting one million LoyalCoin members by 2019,' Palacios informed us.

If successful, they will certainly be one of the shining stars of the blockchain loyalty industry.

TapCoin by Hooch

www.tapcoin.net

Hooch is an existing hospitality perks app with over 200,000 users who currently enjoy discounts at over 100,000 hotels, restaurants and bars across the US. TapCoin by Hooch takes the concept one step further by integrating blockchain and rewarding members with 5-10 per cent back in TapCoin, a cryptotoken which can be redeemed on bookings at hotels, restaurant credits and gift cards including Amazon and Starbucks.

Stacey Lyons, Marketing Director, Loyalty & Reward Co, interviewed Tap by Hooch CEO & Co-founder Lin Dai to find out more about the benefits they see in using blockchain as part of their loyalty program design. 'Blockchain provides the ability to manage millions of micro-transactions efficiently,' said Dai. 'Brands from hospitality to retail can reach millions of consumers and encourage them to take an action by paying them a small amount in digital tokens, which previously was nearly impossible to do efficiently via fiat. Every consumer has a blockchain wallet that becomes their identifier, data is encrypted and sensitive personal information such as name is no longer needed, as smart contracts automatically execute when criteria is met. How the consumers use their rewarded tokens can be trackable, providing transparency and accountability back to brands.'

TapCoin are considering a security token offering in 2019.

Liven

www.liven.com.au

Liven is a fast food and restaurant payments app co-founded by Melbourne-based Gracie Wong and William Wong. Over 200,000 members are using their app across hundreds of Australian restaurant partners, including major chains such as Mad Mex, Lord Of The Fries, Sumo Salad, Gelato Messina and Roll'd (all major Australian fast food chains). When paying through the app, members earn LVN cryptotoken.

Once earned, LVN can be redeemed at participating restaurants or donated to a range of charities.

Stacey Lyons, Marketing Director, Loyalty & Reward Co, interviewed Founder and CEO William Wong to find our more about their approach. 'Practical implementation of blockchain technology ultimately allows us to do two key things: scale our network, and improve the user experience for all participants involved including users, merchants & charities,' said Wong. 'With traditional infrastructure, we'd have many financial and technical hoops to jump through for our platform to reach a wider audience, and the experience would be clunky. Blockchain is a perfect solution to this. Specifically, having the single digital currency makes the user experience as simple as possible no matter where they are. Blockchain also adds never before seen transparency to the charitable giving in our app, allowing users to see directly where their funds go. Aside from this, it opens the platform up to further tech integrations and innovation for the expansion of our offering.'

At the time of writing, Liven are in the middle of an ICO aiming to raise an unspecified sum reported to be in the tens of millions of dollars.

KeyoCoin

www.keyocoin.com

KeyoCoin aim to 'shift the power in the travel industry from a few big, commission hungry players and put it back in the hands of travellers' using cryptorewards. The 'big, commission hungry players' they refer to are Online Travel Agents (OTA's) which charge large commissions for facilitating hotel bookings.

KeyoCoin claim that when compared to today's travel rewards programs, their program is more universal, non-restrictive, efficient, entertaining, and valuable for consumers. They've created a gamified app called KeyoPass. Travel businesses can promote their services for free on the KeyoCoin marketplace which appears in the app, and purchase KeyoCoin to incentivise and reward their customers. Members can earn Keyocoin when purchasing accommodation, local experiences and transportation, and also when they review their travel experiences. KeyoCoin already cover one hundred cities in seven countries with twelve thousand travel products available. Members can also use the app to request room service or a wake-up call, and access expert recommendations.

To drive engagement, KeyoCoin also host travel challenges in the cities in which they operate. Members can access a map in the KeyoPass app to find challenges, such as *The Monkeying Around Challenge* in Rio De Janeiro, where members are invited to 'Find the *Cachoeira dos Macacos* (Monkey's Waterfall) and film yourself swinging from a branch with the waterfall in the pic or video'. Successful completion of the challenge earns members bonus KeyoCoin.

Stacey Lyons, Marketing Director, Loyalty & Reward Co, interviewed KeyoCoin CEO, Matt Baer.

'The concept for KeyoCoin was born around the start of 2017. Our CTO Matias and I had been working on plans to develop a new kind of travel app for some time. In particular one that would create a more rewarding direct relationship between travellers and the millions of hotels, hostels, restaurants, and local experiences that are so lovingly brought into the world by their founders, yet are so hard to come across where travellers are most likely to look for them: on their mobile. At the time we were looking for a way to turn the revenue model of the big OTA's on its head. Of course the added visibility that OTA's bring travel businesses can be valuable, but 10-30% commission is a bitter pill to swallow, especially when most of the money ends up simply fuel-ling a marketing arms race between the big online brands. It was around this time that blockchain's true capabilities were coming into sharper focus, and we realized three important things; Firstly, that a properly designed rewards plat-form had the potential to incentivize revenue-generating consumer actions for all the businesses that used it. Secondly, that those actions could do more than just drive sales for participating businesses, but also grow awareness of our marketplace organically, and therefore cost-effectively. And thirdly, we realized that rewards points were in essence already a form of digital currency, albeit a centralized one, and so presented an absolutely perfect use case for a crypto-currency. What's more by decentralizing the unit of value, we could do away with all the redemption restrictions of centralized programs. We had found a way to use blockchain technology to create the infrastructure we needed to establish the world's first universal travel rewards platform.'

Having consulted to a number of hotel and travel companies, I can con-firm one of their core strategic challenges is to reduce the commissions they pay to OTA's. OTA's have become essential channels for generating bookings, but they charge very high commissions which erode much of the hotel's margin. Hotels do their best to encourage direct bookings by guests via engagement with their loyalty programs, but these tend to mostly be patronised by guests who are already committed to being loyal to the hotel. The real opportunity is to disrupt the OTAs, which is what KeyoCoin is seeking to achieve.

OTA's are a hot target for new blockchain start-ups with Trippki, GoEureka and Gozo also making plays in this space. It remains to be seen how much the big disruptors such as Expedia, Booking.com, Hotels.com, Trivago, TripAdvisor and Wotif can themselves be disrupted by smaller players offer-ing low or zero commissions to hotels and better rewards to members, but the model certainly has potential and is an important space to watch.

Demand Film

www.demand.film
Cinema patrons have the opportunity to earn cryptocurrency by going to the movies thanks to a new blockchain loyalty program by Demand Film. Demand Film, a cinema-on-demand distributor operating in seven countries,

including the USA, UK and Australia, have launched their own cryptotoken; Screencreds.

Patrons who buy movie tickets, view and share trailers, and write movie reviews via www.demand.film will earn Screencreds, which they can then hold to see if the value rises (pending an exchange listing) or trade for movie tickets, VIP events and other money-can't-buy experiences. They'll also be able to trade on an exchange for other cryptocurrencies. Screencred earn will be based on influence. The more people who see the shared trailer, and the more people that then buy tickets to the screenings, the more Screencreds the member will earn.

Demand Film is a favourite of the indie film scene, providing a cinema platform for niche films which would otherwise struggle to get a big screen showing around the world. The key to Demand Film's success is community. Individuals or groups wishing to organise a showing of a particular movie simply fill in a form on www.demand.film. Demand Film then sort out the details and build a customised screening page. They then support the individual or group to promote the film to their community via social media and other means. And there's no risk; if not enough tickets are sold, the event simply doesn't go ahead. Demand Film has done a superb job in building relationships with major cinema chains, who are delighted for their empty seats to be filled mid-week, which is when most Demand Film screenings are held.

As an international company, having their own cryptotoken provides another advantage for Demand Film; they can pay royalties to filmmakers in Screencreds to reduce costs associated with international transfer fees and exchange rates. It will also mean faster payments for filmmakers, with Demand Film moving from a quarterly payment schedule with fiat currencies to a real-time payment schedule with Screencreds.

EZToken

www.eztoken.io
EZPos Holdings, the owner of EZToken, have a network of over 12,000 retailers using their POS system (mostly in Vietnam), of which one third are already utilising their existing points-based functionality. Seeing an opportunity to replace the points-based model with a cryptotoken program, in early 2018 they ran an ICO and raised US$10 million. The last round of their ICO

raised $6 million in just 41 seconds, a stand-out indicator of the irrational exuberance of the peak of the 2017-2018 bull market.

EZToken Rewards was launched in Brisbane in June 2018. One interesting element of the brand positioning was the total absence of any mention of 'blockchain' or 'cryptocurrency'. The team decided to focus on the member benefits rather than the technology, in the same way that modern websites focus on the user experience and not the HTML sitting behind it. EZToken Rewards is described as 'Shopping rewards you can trade'. The member experience is explained as, 'Shop at participating retailers. Earn EZToken for your spend. Hold and see if the value rises or trade and save at participating retailers.'

Despite a positive and focused launch, which included signing up over forty central-Brisbane retailers, the EZToken price plummeted during the bear market, from a high of US$1.60 at exchange launch to just 0.5 cents in early-2019.

While EZToken can be viewed as a casualty of the persistent 2018-19 bear market, the bigger problem is much more serious; excess liquidity. EZToken, and most of the other cryptotoken loyalty companies, have failed to generate enough demand for their cryptotokens within their loyalty program to soak up the supply provided as part of their ICO. By way of illustration, EZToken sold US$10m of cryptotokens into the market. For the loyalty program to soak up all that supply to stimulate a sustained price increase would require members spending US$200m at retailer partners with 5 % of their spend returned to them in EZToken. While this is a fraction of the member spend enjoyed by major coalition programs, it's an almost impossible feat for a start-up.

So does that mean that cryptotoken loyalty programs are dead? No, but for a start-up to succeed in this space will require partnering with a company or network of companies who can deliver the mass of members and spending opportunities required to rapidly build the demand for the token. A more likely scenario is an established company seizing the initiative and creating their own cryptotoken which can be layered over the top of their existing, engaged customer base, such as TapCoin By Hooch. Another example is Japanese e-commerce giant Rakuten who in early 2018 announced they were planning their Rakuten Coin initiative. Their existing points-based loyalty program has awarded more than US$9 billion worth of points since it first debuted in 2003. Their cryptotoken play is designed as a strategic initiative to attract more international customers and will likely be the biggest blockchain loyalty program in the world if it launches. Certainly the 2018-19 bear market will have given them cause to reconsider.

Another Japanese company who are heading down this path is Line (*www.linecorp.com*), a major messaging app provider with 200 million users. In November 2018, Line CEO Takeshi Idezawa announced they were launching their own cryptocurrency loyalty program. 'The accelerated development of the crypto economy and blockchain technologies has created a wide range of options for new types of businesses. To keep up with these trends, Line has decided to launch our own cryptocurrency and blockchain network. Line intends to be a pioneer in the blockchain/crypto field, using our status as a global mobile platform and a listed company to take the initiative with the first cryptocurrency.'

Unlike most cryptocurrency loyalty plays, instead of conducting an ICO to raise funds, Line are going to airdrop LINK to current customers as compensation for using their Line services, products or completing specific requests. This is incredibly important, as it allows Line to control the amount of cryptocurrency liquidity in the market, which will help them reduce the risk of significant price drops which are a core driver of member disengagement. Unfortunately, this isn't a viable option for most start-ups as they require the funds raised via ICO to build their retailer and member base, although venture capital funding is always an option.

2. A loyalty program powered by an existing cryptocurrency

One viable alternative to creating a new cryptotoken is for a loyalty program operator to use an existing, popular cryptocurrency to reward members, such as Bitcoin, Ether or LiteCoin.

As mentioned earlier, it's incredibly difficult to convince retailers to buy a new loyalty currency to reward their customers with. It's equally hard to convince a customer to become a member. And once the program is up and running, it's difficult to stimulate ongoing engagement with the program.

How is it that the big loyalty programs continue to enjoy such phenomenal success in driving ongoing member engagement from millions of consumers and businesses? Why do people consciously change their shopping behaviour to amass more of their points and miles?

The main reason is they have successfully created *highly desirable* loyalty currencies. While the currencies weren't always highly desirable (i.e. when they were just launched), they have grown to be so in the eyes of the members base who clearly understand and appreciate the value they can unlock (e.g. free flights).

Our world-first blockchain loyalty study at the University of NSW in 2017 (detailed in Chapter 5) showed Ether cryptocurrency was significantly more desirable than popular loyalty points amongst participants. While this may appear to be an argument for cryptotokens over loyalty points, it's actually a more plausible argument for desirable currencies over unknown currencies. In many ways, Ether more closely resembles a popular loyalty currency than a new cryptotoken. This is because, just like frequent flyer points, Ether is widely-known and drives extensive engagement (over US$1bn daily average trading volume). Ether is a known product, a brand. It's liquid, easily tradeable and yes, highly desirable.

Thus, companies looking to build a blockchain loyalty program should include in their list of considerations the utilisation of a major cryptocurrency as an alternative to creating their own cryptotoken.

In many ways, major cryptocurrencies deliver significantly more benefits than most popular loyalty currencies. While desirable, points and miles are expensive for retailers to buy, are restricted in what they can be redeemed on, and they expire. They also tend to be part of relatively localised programs. In contrast, major cryptocurrencies are cost-effective to buy (no excessive margins earned by the loyalty program operator), they can be bought and sold all around the world and they never expire.

Blockchain loyalty absolutely has a role to play in reinventing the loyalty industry, but only if it delivers something which in the eyes of members is more appealing than what they can currently access. While cryptotokens have the potential to play a part, a genuine opportunity is using the major cryptocurrencies to reward loyalty and drive deeper engagement. This is an area which is likely to see significant growth.

Two examples of companies operating in this space are both using online affiliate marketing networks to help consumers earn cryptocurrencies. Lolli (*www.lolli.com*) in the US allows members to shop online at over 500 retailers and earn Bitcoin. Bitcoin Rewards (*www.bitcoinrewards.com*) allows shoppers in 6 different countries to earn Bitcoin Cash.

A variation on this approach is loyalty programs allowing members to redeem their points or miles for popular cryptocurrencies. Persuade Loyalty (*www.persuadeloyalty.com*) have developed CryptoRewards Exchange which is designed to integrate with loyalty platforms to allow members to redeem points for Bitcoin, Ether and Litecoin, something members of EZ Rent-A-Car in the US can do using EZ Money, their loyalty currency.

3. Many loyalty programs powered by multiple new cryptoto-kens on a single platform

Several blockchain loyalty companies are trying to solve a different problem to the early cryptotoken loyalty players; the issue of interchangeability. One of the core issues cited by many loyalty industry observers is that consumers join multiple loyalty programs, earn small amounts of points across them, but not enough in a single program to gain anything of value. As a result the points expire, the member becomes disengaged, and the loyalty program has achieved nothing other than dis-loyalty.

The approach being taken by a number of start-ups is a blockchain loyalty platform which supports multiple individual loyalty programs.

Under this model, a large number of retailers can have their own unique, branded cryptotoken with a fixed value which they can use to reward their members. For the member, the cryptotokens aren't discernible from points or miles, except for one important feature; the members can choose to redeem their cryptotokens with the retailer they earned them from, but they can also redeem them with any of the other retailers connected to the platform or even swap them for the underlying platform cryptocurrency and sell them on an exchange.

If they're shopping at multiple retailers, the member now has the opportunity to accumulate their cryptotokens to access a bigger reward, in much the same way as if they were participating in a coalition loyalty program such as a frequent flyer program.

Let's look at some of the companies playing in this space:

GATCOIN

www.gatcoin.io

GATCOIN (Global Awards Token Coin) has valued the total loyalty points and miles market at US$320 billion worldwide but perceive a lack of customer utilisation. They attribute this to the inflexible nature of retail points and shopping incentives, meaning users aren't easily able to transfer, exchange or sell them to other users. Their vision is a unified world of rewards, where consumers no longer have to join multiple loyalty, rewards and point programs and carry many cards and apps.

GATCOIN's platform allows retailers to convert their existing loyalty currency into a branded retailer token. These can be redeemed with retailers or freely traded for GAT cryptotokens. Customers can transfer GATCOIN to any exchange in the world and trade them for fiat or other cryptocurrencies and tokens. GATCOIN believes the ability to convert incentive points into real money frees the customer from any single points ecosystem and allows consumers to achieve 100 per cent utilisation of their disparate incentives.

In early 2018, GATCOIN successfully raised US$14.5 million via ICO. The initial exchange price went as high as 9 cents before dropping steadily to arrive at 0.1 cents in early-2019 with virtually no daily trading volume, indicating GATCOIN has been unsuccessful in attracting the retailer engagement required as part of their strategic vision.

Momentum Protocol

www.momentumtoken.io

Using the Momentum Protocol, companies can convert their existing loyalty program to, or create a new loyalty program on, a blockchain-based standardised environment and even launch their own cryptotoken. The standard removes the technical and operational barriers for consumers to easily swap their tokens from one loyalty program to the next, thus providing much needed liquidity. For companies, it means an opportunity to easily create alliances with other companies that follow the same standard, which increases their addressable audience substantially, and gives them a platform that provides them with much better data insights, not only regarding consumer behaviour in their own eco-system, but also outside it.

I spoke with Kees de Vos, CEO of Momentum Protocol about their platform and its features. 'The blockchain was a natural technology choice to form the foundation for the Momentum platform,' he said. 'To start with, loyalty points are a virtual currency and it has been proven that the best technology available to move these virtual currencies in a secure, transparent, global and cost efficient manner is blockchain. Other virtual currencies like Bitcoin, are proving this day in, day out. In addition to being a perfect, global ledger, it also provides an immutable transaction record, which we not only use for the processing of loyalty points, but also to manage access to the consumers' user profile for example. This instils trust in the system and gives control over their user data back to the consumer.'

'When companies join the Momentum platform, they will be able to launch their own token - e.g. Hungry Jacks will reward their customers in Hungry Jacks Tokens and Qantas will use the Qantas Token. Each token will have its own, fixed value, rather than something that goes up and down due to market speculation. This would not be acceptable by a lot of retailers. The Momentum Token is a token that is solely required to get access to the system (a payment token for participating companies) and is also instrumental in providing a single reference of value to enable global transfer of tokens (a utility token, in this role). The Momentum Token will be the token that is publicly available and which may change in value due to the market's demand.'

In early-2019, Momentum Protocol were in the middle of a private-ICO, having already reached their soft cap target of €2.5m in 2018. From their existing company, MobileBridge (*www.mobilebridge.com*) they already have a strong, global partner network to help increase their reach and have been working with several partners in each category to kick-start their growth.

DigitalBits

www.digitalbits.io

DigitalBits is an open-source project supporting the adoption of blockchain technology by enterprises. The technology enables enterprises to tokenise assets on the decentralised DigitalBits blockchain; transfer & trade those tokenised assets on-chain; and enables fast payments and remittances.

DigitalBits appears to be making good progress in onboarding retailers and other partners. Since launch in mid-2018, the platform has onboarded leading Stellar wallet Lobstr, customer engagement platform Caddle, cloud provider Cogeco Peer 1 and Metalyfe blockchain browser. Led by CEO Al Burgio, they've also attracted a number of heavy weight investors including Bloq, Arcadia Crypto Ventures, Blocktower and Rivetz.

While being able to earn a loyalty currency with one retailer and spend it with another sounds ideal for consumers, it might not be as appealing for retailers. Some retailers may feel reluctant to join a loyalty program where the value they provide to members can be redeemed outside their business, in the same way major loyalty programs block the ability for members to redeem beyond their walled garden. The major loyalty programs often offer exclusivity to retail partners to address this issue. For example, they may only allow one telecommunications company or one supermarket to join the program and shut their competitors out. Cryptotoken loyalty companies are likely to follow the same strategy once (or if) they manage to achieve scale.

4. A security token supported by a loyalty program

Blockchain loyalty approaches have for the most part been dominated by *utility tokens*, which within the loyalty industry are cryptotokens issued to fund development of the loyalty program, and can be redeemed on goods or services offered by program partners. The likes of EZToken, Incent, LoyalCoin and CampusCoin are all examples of loyalty utility tokens.

Utility tokens deliver a range of benefits for the program operator, the primary one being that they can be created and sold to raise funds without the need to sacrifice company equity. This has made ICO's a thoroughly exciting and highly lucrative crowdfunding vehicle over the past few years.

But easily raising funds using utility tokens came to a sudden halt in mid-2018 with many ICOs struggling to hit soft caps. One didn't need to search too far to find the culprit; the current and persistent 2018-19 bear market. That being said, some may argue the culprit was an excess of ICOs not delivering on their promise, which triggered the bear market. Certainly, it would be a tough job to convince someone to invest in a cryptotoken loyalty program ICO in 2019 when most of the earlier programs have failed or are failing. One thing is certain, the days of irrational exuberance regarding ICO investments appear to be over, at least for the time being.

A good example to illustrate the market sentiment is EZToken. The team raised US$10m in January via ICO, including raising US$6m in around 41 seconds in their last round, a staggering feat. Today, EZToken would be lucky to raise US$1m (if they could raise at all), with the appetite for ventures selling an idea without an MVP all but dead. Meanwhile the EZToken price (EZT), which peaked at US$1.60, is worth just 0.5c on exchanges.

So where does the future lie? Many industry advisors are looking squarely at *security tokens*. Unlike utility tokens, which confer no rights on the holder other than ownership and the ability to sell on a participating exchange, a security token can provide the investor with dividends, equity, profit share rights, buy back rights and voting rights, making them potentially more valuable and thus more desirable.

A general example of a security token is one provided by Blockchain Capital. They raised US$10m via ICO selling their own security token and now distribute their trading profits to their security token holders, something a company which distributed utility tokens wouldn't do.

This is of significant interest to the loyalty industry. While security tokens themselves cannot be provided to members of a loyalty program as a reward currency because of licensing and disclosure issues, a loyalty program can be designed around security tokens to make them more attractive to acquire and retain.

An example of a non-blockchain security which has used this approach in the past is Coles-Myer, a now-disbanded Australian supermarket and department store organisation. Back in the day, shareholders of Coles-Myer were provided with the Coles-Myer Shareholder Card, which entitled them to benefits including a 10 per cent discount at Myer and a 5 per cent discount at

Coles. Launched in 1993, the card was so popular that by 2001 shareholder numbers had swelled from some 68,000 to 580,000, including large numbers of 'mum and dad' investors. This successfully kept the share price value inflated and also reduced the risk of a hostile take-over.

This provides a neat model for a new type of blockchain loyalty program; one where security token holders can be provided with the opportunity to access additional rewards, thereby increasing the likelihood of accumulation and retention. This, in turn, can lead to increased demand for a reduced tradeable supply, which has the potential to drive the price higher on exchanges.

It even provides an opportunity for a new approach for utility cryptotoken loyalty programs. Consider a company that wishes to raise funds to expand. Instead of running an ICO, it can choose to run an STO, providing investors with security tokens. The company can then use some of the funds raised to launch a loyalty program where members are rewarded with a branded utility cryptotoken. The cryptotoken can later be floated on an exchange without the need for the company to run an ICO, avoiding the cost and effort associated with an ICO and enabling better management of liquidity.

Security tokens are an incredibly new area, and one with much promise. Future editions of *Blockchain Loyalty* will cover security tokens and loyalty more extensively as the market evolves. Feature articles will also be posted on *www.blockchainloyalty.io*

CHAPTER 7

THE CRYPTOTOKEN LOYALTY PROGRAM COMMERCIAL MODEL

In Chapter 6 we explored four different approaches to utilising cryptocurrencies and cryptotokens within loyalty programs. We'll now explore the commercial advantages which can be provided by creating a new cryptotoken for use within a loyalty program. The underlying commercial model of a cryptotoken loyalty program involves a fundamental element: *currency scarcity*.

A company running a loyalty program offering points and miles can create as many points and miles as they have demand for. Provided they're able to cover the value of those points or miles when the member redeems them, the amount they can create is unlimited.

With cryptotoken loyalty programs, the strategy is to create a finite amount of cryptotokens. The program operator will declare in their whitepaper the total number of tokens which will be created (or pre-mined) and no more will ever be made. This creates the conditions for scarcity, the importance of which will be discussed throughout this chapter.

To understand the commercial differences between points and miles programs and cryptotoken loyalty programs, let's compare the two using economic models.

Most people are surprised to learn that loyalty programs can actually be profitable for the business operating the program. They view loyalty programs as giving something to customers and automatically conclude they must therefore be a cost to the business. Certainly, many retail programs run this way but the big coalition loyalty programs can be hugely profitable, with their annual revenue in the billions and profits in the hundreds of millions. How can these sorts of profits manifest?

Let's consider a frequent flyer program. Initially, they were created to reward the airline's most loyal customers but soon after being created the airlines realised they had given birth to something very valuable: a highly desirable currency. Hotels and car rental firms quickly started partnering with the airlines and over time this expanded to banks, insurance companies, retailers and many other industries. These companies realised they could gain a competitive edge in their market by offering the frequent flyer program's points or miles to their customers, who would choose to shop with them to increase their loyalty currency accumulation, moving their account balance more quickly towards a free flight.

The new opportunity for the airlines was twofold. Firstly, customers were more likely to remain loyal to the airline if they could gain free flights by accumulating the loyalty currency. Secondly, the airlines realised they could generate incremental profits by selling the points to their earn partners.

Consider this situation: a member of a frequent flyer program spends $1,000 with a participating retailer. They swipe their membership card and earn 1,000 points. The frequent flyer program will invoice the retailer for the cost of the points at a rate of 1.5 cents per point, costing the retailer $15. That's right. The retailers who reward their customers with points from a frequent flyer program must pay the program for the points. While frequent flyer programs started as loyalty programs, they've now morphed into 'points-selling' businesses.

When the member chooses to redeem those points in the future, the frequent flyer program assigns a lower value to the points. Although they charged the retailer 1.5 cents per point, the value per point for the customer when they redeem them may be just 1 cent. Thus in our example, for each point sold and then redeemed, the frequent flyer program earns 0.5 cents. This may not sound like a lot but a big frequent flyer program can sell hundreds of billions of points each year, generating massive profits. In the case of our example, the frequent flyer program has sold the points for $15 but it has cost them $10 when they're redeemed, earning them $5 profit on a single transaction.

If the member doesn't use the points and they expire, the frequent flyer program banks the full 1.5 cents (or $15 in our example). Most frequent flyer programs have anywhere from 5 per cent to 20 per cent of their total points volume expire each year, contributing significantly to underlying profits.

The frequent flyer program also earns interest. When the points are sold the program operator must defer enough revenue to a holding account to cover the cost of the future reward (or liability). For example, if a member earns $50 of points, the operator must set aside $50 in a separate account, ensuring they have enough revenue allocated to cover the value of the reward when the member redeems them. The bank pays interest on this deferred revenue balance. A deferred revenue holding of several billion dollars is not unusual for a large coalition loyalty program.

From a pure economic modelling viewpoint, the supply and demand graph is defined by a perfectly horizontal supply line:

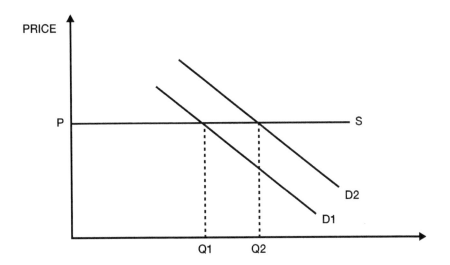

An increase in demand (from D1 to D2) for the loyalty currency translates directly into an increase in quantity (from Q1 to Q2), with no upward or downward pressure on the price. The frequent flyer program simply creates as much additional points or miles as required, deposits them into the members' account and invoices the retail partner. They literally have a licence to print digital money.

This ignores the ability for the frequent flyer program to adjust the price and value of the currency to optimise their profit margin, which they do very effectively. Depending on what reward a member redeems their points on, the value they receive for their points is likely to be different. For example, points redeemed on a flight may deliver a value of 1 cent per point but if redeemed on a gift card they may deliver a value of 0.75 cents, while a toaster may give just 0.5 cents value. This pricing strategy is designed to both guide the member to redeem their loyalty currency on a reward which keeps the cash flow within the business (i.e. free flights) and take advantage of wholesale margins on third party products to boost profits.

The frequent flyer program will also try to sell their points for as much as possible. While our example uses the cost of 1.5 cents to the retailer, other retailers may pay 2 cents or 2.5 cents or even 3 cents, depending on their level of negotiating skills. Other retailers may agree to provide multiple points for each dollar spent by the member, so they end up spending 3 to 6 per cent of their total revenue on points or even more. The strategies used to maximise profits are incredibly sophisticated.

Now let us consider the model for a cryptotoken loyalty program.

The operator creates a finite amount of a loyalty cryptotoken; let's call them *Tokenz* (TKZ) and let's assume that one billion are created. A smart contract is set-up on the blockchain platform preventing any more TKZ ever being created. The loyalty company run an ICO and sell a percentage of them at a set price to anyone who wants to buy them; in our example, 200 million are sold at a set price of 10 cents per TKZ, generating $20 million of start-up capital. A further 100 million are distributed to the project team, business owners, early investors and advisors. This leaves 700 million TKZ as a company reserve.

At the end of the ICO, the loyalty company distributes the TKZ to the cryptocurrency wallets of the many ICO investors and floats TKZ on a digital trading exchange (or several). They can now be traded by participants of the ICO, as well as speculators who choose to buy and sell on the open market.

The operator then launches the loyalty program. With the right approach, they'll have a network of retailers who participate in rewarding their customers with TKZ and accepting TKZ as a payment method. When a member of the program transacts with the retailer, the retailer will contribute a percentage of the transaction to cover the cost of the TKZ in exactly the same way as if they were buying points or miles from a frequent flyer program.

But here's where things differ between the two models: rather than the loyalty company creating new points to provide to the member, the loyalty company takes the contribution from the retailer and purchases a TKZ allocation from the digital trading exchange. This creates on-market demand for TKZ and if there's enough retailers and engaged members involved in the program, it will create strong and sustained demand. Following our example; a member spends $1,000 with a participating retailer. They swipe their membership card and earn $10 of TKZ, which are purchased at the market rate. If the market rate is $1, they'll receive 10 TKZ and if the market rate is $2 they'll receive 5 TKZ. Unlike the points model, the loyalty company doesn't make a large margin on the transaction meaning a greater amount of value is transferred from the retailer to the member. The program operator can also charge a transaction fee on TKZ which are earned and redeemed to generate some revenue for the company. They should apply a fee to the transaction, although anything excessive is likely to be contentious from a retailer and member perspective. Once again the market will work to regulate the value structure.

This upfront transaction is very different to a points and miles program which requires the deferral of revenue to cover future liabilities. This will appeal to some companies, who don't want to take on the complexity of deferred revenue loyalty program models. Other companies might prefer to defer the revenue, rather than wear the immediate cost of the reward upfront. It is something which needs consideration by companies when determining whether a cryptotoken loyalty program is right for them.

When a member redeems TKZ, the reverse applies. The loyalty company takes the amount of TKZ the member wants to redeem (or the dollar amount of TKZ they wish to redeem) and sells them on the exchange. They then provide the fiat currency to the retailer, less a transaction fee.

Here's what the economic model looks like for a blockchain loyalty program:

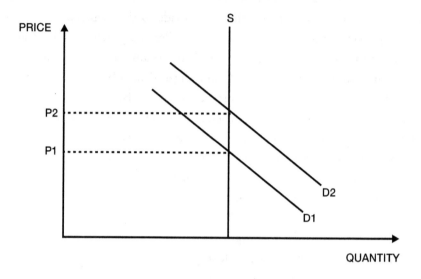

The vertical supply curve is the exact opposite of the horizontal points and miles supply curve for a points and miles program. This is because the total supply of TKZ is finite (set at one billion TKZ) and no more will ever be created. Thus, if demand increases for TKZ (movement from D1 to D2) via growth in retailer participation, growth in the member base and/or member spend, or via an increase in speculative buying behaviour on the exchange, the price will subsequently rise (from P1 to P2).

Scarcity is the first lesson that economics students around the world learn. It's why diamonds are worth more than dirt and is the fundamental economic theory underpinning a cryptotoken loyalty program.

Consider the profit potential of such a program: with 300 million TKZ in circulation at a launch value of $30 million, the operator's reserve is valued at $70 million. This is $70 million that has been created from - essentially - nothing. TKZ didn't exist until the operator created them and it cost them nothing. Now consider if the value of TKZ rises above 10 cents due to a demand increase. At 20 cents per TKZ, the reserve is worth $140 million. At 50 cents per TKZ, the reserve is worth $350 million. At $2 per TKZ, the reserve is worth $1.4 billion and the blockchain loyalty start-up is officially a "unicorn".

Managed wisely, the reserve can provide massive value akin to cash-in-bank which the loyalty company can draw on over many years to grow the program and build additional revenue streams.

Of course, the opposite is also true. If the value of TKZ drops to 5 cents, or 2 cents, or 0.01 cents, then the value of the reserve plummets. This is the actual reality facing most cryptotoken loyalty programs around the world today, because they've not been able to generate sufficient demand within the program to soak up the excess supply. That isn't to say the model is flawed. The pure economics is still valid, but it will require an extensive retailer network and engaged member database to generate the level of demand required to grow the cryptotoken value in a sustained way, something very difficult for a start-up to achieve.

One advantage cryptotoken loyalty companies have over most other blockchain companies is the ability to generate most of the demand for the cryptotoken within the loyalty ecosystem rather than on trading exchanges. Most blockchain companies have created a cryptotoken as a way to raise funds via an ICO, without a genuine need to have their own cryptotoken. For example, there are many blockchain companies which force users to buy their cryptotoken to transact on their platform, even though it would be relatively easy to allow them to use fiat or other cryptocurrencies. It is an attempt to force the necessity of the existence of a currency which has no need to exist. Loyalty cryptotokens are necessary to the company's operation; the program can't run without them, and if the program operator is successful in signing up retailers and members, the demand created will build a solid foundation for the value which will be relatively impervious to market sentiment.

Outside of their cryptotoken reserve, the loyalty company can also generate revenue from transaction fees and a new revenue stream from blockchain marketing, which is covered in Chapter 15.

While most blockchain companies will do everything they can to send their cryptocurrency price 'to the moon' (a crypto term for a large price increase) as quickly as possible, this is not the right strategy for a cryptotoken loyalty program. A measured and consistent price rise is likely to be more effective in growing and maintaining member engagement. This is because too rapid a price rise will present the risk of a rapid decent which has the potential to generate disengagement. As discussed earlier, wild price fluctuations are arguably the single biggest challenge facing a cryptotoken loyalty program operator.

Imagine a scenario where the cryptotoken value quickly increases from 10 cents to $1 in value (as happened with Incent during the 2017-2018 bull market). For those members who have already earned a reasonable accumulation of the currency as part of their transactions with participating retailers this would be a fantastic event, particularly if they take the opportunity to redeem. However, for new members who are just starting to earn, the accumulation is at a high price versus historical averages. If the price suddenly declines, the value they have accumulated is reduced and they may not see any benefit in continuing their engagement with the program.

This may also be the case for long term members who maintain their holding in the hope the price will go even higher. If it rises too quickly it may trigger speculative sell behaviour, causing it to decline rapidly. Those members will be taken on the emotional rollercoaster known well by share traders the world over. This is a very different experience to earning points and miles and one that may be too much to bear for some members. Backlash and negative publicity may ensue which could damage the brand of the both the program and its retail partners.

So what can be done to help deliver a measured and consistent cryptotoken price rise?

The first step is getting the *tokenomics* right. According to Ennis et al,[22] tokenomics covers 'the set of all economic activity that has been generated through the creation of cryptotokens.'

As discussed, the biggest challenge many blockchain companies face regarding the value of their cryptotoken is that they don't have an eco-system which is effective in generating sufficient demand for all the tokens in circulation. This is exacerbated by the fact they likely sold too many tokens at ICO in order to raise as much money as possible. As a result, most of the buy and sell activity for their cryptotoken takes place on exchanges which means the value of their token is almost entirely dependent on market sentiment. With a market as volatile as cryptocurrency trading, price swings have been seen to be considerable.

The recommended strategy for a cryptotoken loyalty company is to limit

---

22 https://www.coindesk.com/three-definitions-tokenomics/

the amount of tokens held by investors and aim for the majority of buy and sell behaviour to occur within the program via earn and redemption transactions. Thus, if the speculative market pumps or dumps, the loyalty program token value is somewhat insulated because the average member isn't trading, but accumulating for a future reward. As established earlier, a cryptotoken loyalty company has a greater chance of survival if most of the buy/sell behaviour happens within the program, not as speculative trading on exchanges. It is also critical that the demand for tokens within the program is greater than the supply held by active traders.

Quality commercial modelling will allow the loyalty company to ascertain the minimum amount of cash they need to raise via ICO to survive the first couple of years (of if they can avoid an ICO altogether), how many members they need to acquire, how much each member needs to spend per annum and what percentage of revenue retailers need to return to members in order to generate enough demand for tokens within the program. This will lead to a sustained and sustainable cryptotoken price rise and one which is resistant to downward price pressure from speculative selling.

The outcome from this should be a decision by the loyalty company to aim for a much smaller ICO raise (or none at all), so less cryptotokens are injected into the hands of investors/traders. The company always has the option to sell more cryptotokens if required. Another consideration is to try to direct most of the cryptotokens into the hands of a small number of investors who the company can work with to ensure they only sell at strategic times (difficult but still possible).

A further option is to delay the launch of the token on an exchange for 6-12 months after the conclusion of the ICO so the loyalty company can gain some traction with the program prior to the advent of speculative trading. This includes building a participating retailer network, recruiting the first wave of members, injecting cryptotokens into the accounts of members and generally building demand for cryptotokens through the program. Thus, when the cryptotoken does hit the exchange, the loyalty company has a fully working program with lots of small buy orders hitting the exchange to support the price. The downside of this approach is ICO investors will not appreciate a lag in the cryptotoken hitting exchanges, as their investment money is tied up in an asset they cannot sell.

It is also worth considering using loyalty theory to encourage investors to hold their cryptotoken allocation for as long as possible. This may be in the form of a time-based loyalty bonus. For example, if an ICO investor holds their cryptotokens for one year, they may receive an additional 5% of cryptotokens as a reward.

With the creation of a cryptotoken and the formation of a sizeable reserve, the loyalty company operator may also choose to maintain a cash and cryptotoken reserve, then use that reserve to smooth out the price fluctuations of their coin via strategic buy and sell behaviour. This approach can be compared to similar strategies used by a reserve bank or central bank managing the exchange rate of their country's fiat currency. It can also be compared to a publicly listed company buying and selling their own shares to manage share price volatility. It is important to note that most countries have laws against market manipulation, which is a 'deliberate attempt to interfere with the free and fair operation of the market and create artificial, false or misleading appearances with respect to the price of, or market for, a product, security, commodity or currency.'[23] Thus, any approach which involves buying or selling a reserve to affect the value of a cryptotoken needs to abide with the laws of the countries in which that cryptotoken is traded. An example of good practice in the crypto-markets is action taken by DeepBrainChain who, in March 2018, announced to the market they were intending to re-purchase 40 million DBC cryptotokens as a method to increase the value of non-repurchased tokens.[24] Suffice to say, this is not intended to be viewed as financial or commercial advice and any company planning to utilise this approach is advised to seek financial and legal guidance.

---

23 Wikipedia

24 https://neonewstoday.com/general/ deepbrain-chain-announce-repurchase-of-dbc-tokens/

CHAPTER 8

CRYPTOTOKEN LOYALTY PROGRAM TAX AND LEGAL CONSIDERATIONS

*This chapter was contributed by Michael
Bacina (Partner, Piper Alderman)*

BLOCKCHAIN BASED LOYALTY programs are still in their infancy, and as is often the case, the law lags behind the pace of technological change. With strong interest and significant sums flowing into the blockchain ecosystem in recent years, as well as the rise of Initial Coin Offerings (ICOs), regulators around the world have been moving to protect consumers (and in some cases investors) from unlicensed security offerings, misleading or deceptive conduct, the risk of money laundering/terrorism financing and of course looking to ensure tax is calculated (and paid) properly.

The Australian approach to loyalty schemes, as well as to tax treatment of cryptocurrencies, is instructive in considering the regulatory risks of blockchain based loyalty programs and the deployment of same. Developments in this area are occurring swiftly, so any project should ensure they engage competent legal counsel to ensure compliance with local laws where the loyalty scheme is to operate.

1. Financial licencing

Fundamentally, all loyalty programs bear a strong similarity to the offer of financial services. In the blockchain context this usually arises in a few ways. Firstly, where a loyalty system permits points/credits or tokens (hereafter we will use 'points' for convenience) to be transferred between users or in payment for goods or services, which could be providing a money transmitter service or, in Australia, be a 'non-cash payment facility'. Where fiat to cryptocurrency conversions occur, requirements to register under anti-money laundering legislation may arise (see commentary on AML/CTF below) and of course running an ICO to pre-sell loyalty points runs the risk of being considered to be the offer of an investment contract/managed investment scheme.

A 'non-cash payment facility' occurs where a person permits payments to be made other than by the physical delivery of Australian or foreign currency in notes or coins. Those offering a non-cash payment facility in Australia must either hold an Australian Financial Services Licence (**AFSL**) or fall within an exemption. Two such exemptions to the *Corporations Act 2001 (Cth)* are operating a "low-value" non-cash payment facility (if certain reduced disclosures are met) or where a facility is a loyalty scheme.

In order to qualify as a loyalty scheme, an offering must meet the following criteria:

a. The dominant purpose of the scheme must be to promote the purchase of goods from, or the use of services of, the party operating the scheme or another business; and

b. A person using the scheme must be allocated points (or tokens) as a result of the purchase of goods from, or the use of the services of, the party operating the scheme or another person; and

c. The points (or tokens) allocated in the program can be used to make a payment or part payment for goods or services or to obtain some other benefit; and

d. The program is not a component of another financial product.

A traditional loyalty system could simply replace their current databasing by using a token driven system, and should have little difficulty complying with the above requirements. The greater challenge arises where a greater element of decentralisation occurs, such as through the use of masternodes or other incentivised users of the platform, or where secondary trading of reward points is offered.

While many airline program loyalty schemes have permitted the transfer and sale of points for a long time, and permit top-up points purchases, selling points as a pre-sale of goods or services may not meet compliance with the second limb of the test in Australia, as the points may not be arising from the *'purchase of goods or services'* but rather from a transaction to acquire the points themselves with a future purchase of goods or services with the points.

Another important requirement for exclusion from licensing requirements is that the points are not a component of another financial product. The *Corporations Act* has an expansive definition of what is a 'financial product' and many loyalty programs, including blockchain based loyalty programs, could fall within this definition, particularly if the tokens representing points are offered for sale prior to the points being usable within a platform, or if they are seen as a form of fundraising. The offer of a financial product in Australia carries with it specific licensing and disclosure obligations which can be expensive and onerous, and significant penalties apply when these obligations are not met.

Licensing requirements are most likely to arise where the offer of points is made before a loyalty platform is functional. In Australia, ASIC's INFO225 guidance document suggests that many Initial Coin Offerings would be characterised as managed investment schemes, which are treated as 'financial products' and have licensing and disclosure obligations. In the USA, Mr Jay Clayton, Chairman of the Security and Exchanges Commission in the USA has indicated ICOs need to comply with securities laws.

However, the UK in early 2019 has taken a different approach, with a Financial Conduct Authority consultation paper suggesting the FCA will only treat as securities those tokens which provide explicit security like features such as revenue or dividend sharing, or which actually represent ownership of an underlying asset. That paper indicated that the FCA considers so called "utility tokens" akin to crowdfunding outside of regulations, such as that offered by Kickstarter, Indiegogo and others. Loyalty points offered for sale within a loyalty scheme, so long as they don't provide any ownership of underlying assets or revenue/profit sharing or dividend rights, may have a strong likelihood of being considered "utility tokens" and hence not be regulated in the UK if this line of thinking is adopted at law. It will remain to be seen if the consultation paper becomes a formal guidance in the UK or adopted in other countries, such as Australia. It seems unlikely that the SEC in the USA will follow the UK's lead on this point given enforcement action by the SEC to date.

2. Taxation implications

Another area which has attracted early interest from governments around the world is how to manage the taxation of transactions involving cryptotokens. As tokens fundamentally represent some kind of contract when a transaction is entered into, the main analysis when considering whether and how tax will apply is to consider just what a party is contracting for in a transaction and how that transaction is treated under the tax laws of the jurisdiction in which it occurred.

In Australia, an amendment to the the Goods and Services Tax (**GST**) laws provided an exemption from GST which appears designed to apply to Bitcoin. Specifically, GST was exempted from "digital currency" from 1 July 2017. The tax law defines digital currency as a 'digital unit of value that has all of the following characteristics':

- It is fully interchangeable with another unit of the same digital currency for the purpose of payment;

- It can be provided as payment for any types of purchases;

- It is generally available to the public free of any substantial restrictions;

- It is not denominated in any country's currency;

- The value is not derived from or dependent on anything else; and

- It does not give an entitlement or privileges to receive something else.

The ATO has stated that it will not consider loyalty points issued by retailers that can only be redeemed for products or services specified by a loyalty scheme to be digital currency for GST purposes. Similarly, the ATO has released guidance and a ruling concerning the tax treatment of loyalty schemes which appears well settled. Simply because a loyalty scheme is blockchain is no compelling reason for tax treatment to be different. However, an important distinction may arise where the loyalty points are tradeable, in which case the holders of the points should ensure they are keeping adequate records if their purchase or sale of the tokens is other than in connection with personal or domestic use. It must also be recognised that cryptocurrencies are considered to be a nuanced asset class, which can be utilised and applied in ways that other assets are not able to be applied. Cryptocurrencies also have unique components, such as forks. A fork is a change to the covert protocol in the relevant blockchain, and requires all nodes that are linked to the blockchain, to update to the new protocol software and adopt that new version moving forward. At this moment, there are two available strands of forks; a hard fork and a soft fork. A hard fork changes the protocol code entirely, creating a fresh version of the blockchain, and a soft fork is merely an update to the blockchain protocol. Examples of forks that have occured within the past 2 years include; the "Segwit" fork which occurred in August 2017, the Bitcoin Cash fork, and the Bitcoin Gold fork.

Where new cryptocurrency cash is involved, for example, when Bitcoin holders receive Bitcoin Cash as a result of the hard fork, the ATO states that taxpayers do not derive ordinary income or make a capital gain at that time. However, the capital gain will only come about when the newly made cryptocurrency is disposed of. The ATO stated that it is unlikely that the new cryptocurrency will be stored as a personal use asset, and hence, will not be entitled to the personal use asset exemption. It should be noted however, that the ATO guidance at this time is not legally binding upon the ATO as the law in this area is extremely nuanced, and has not been well established. It is likely that in the future this position will be challenged, as the existing and new assets (Bitcoin and Bitcoin Cash for example) will be classified as the same type and therefore be ascribed as identical within the holder's statement of financial position.

3. AML/CTF obligations

Obligations in regards to Anti-Money Laundering and Counter-Terrorism Financing (**AML/CTF**) are in place to ensure that businesses in Australia and around the world do not engage in money laundering and the financing of terrorism. In Australia, the principal legislation is the *Anti-Money Laundering/ Counter-Terrorism Funding Act 2006* (**AML/CTF Act**), and its purpose is to "bring Australia into line with international best practice to deter money laundering and terrorism financing." This is important, as Australian AML/

CTF laws must remain comparable to such laws in a foreign country. Effective implementation of AML/CTF laws in Europe such as the *Directive (EU) 2015/849 on preventing the use of the financial system for money laundering or terrorist financing,* and the *Bank Secrecy Act* 1970 in America, provide for an efficient and expansive process for reporting entities to combat corruption domestically and overseas.

The AML/CTF Act applies where a person is providing a 'designated service'. For the most part it is unlikely that a loyalty program operator is providing a 'designated service' and the definition of digital currency under that Act should normally not apply to loyalty points. However, where the loyalty points are represented by a form of digital currency, and the platform operator is providing an exchange between fiat currency and that digital currency, in Australia (and likely other countries) a 'designated service' will be very likely being provided and compliance with the AML/CTF Act will be required. Such compliance in Australia will include registering with AUSTRAC as a Digital Currency Exchange and developing an AML/CTF Program and appropriate supporting policies, training and guidelines for employees.

There are substantial fines and custodial penalties for failing to comply with the AML/CTF Act and it is expected in future that the Financial Action Task Force (FATF) will be seeking to extend AML/CTF compliance to include digital currency to digital currency conversions, which may render current crypto-centric loyalty schemes the subject of more onerous compliance. The best strategy at present is to have a comprehensive Know Your Customer system in place, which may also assist in gathering data for a loyalty program by ensuring that a customer is properly identified when they are interacting with the loyalty program. Dovetailing into this is a need to have a comprehensive privacy consent and disclosure to address compliance with the *Privacy Act* (in Australia) and the *General Data Protection Regulation* (in Europe) which goes beyond the scope of this chapter.

4. Misleading or deceptive conduct considerations

Regulators across different jurisdictions have been heavily focused on the nature of the token offerings, in particular, the contents of whitepapers and advertising material published and discussed on social media platforms such as Telegram, Twitter and Medium. Regardless of the jurisdiction that loyalty tokens are issued in, unfair or deceptive conduct and representations are strongly condemned by regulators.

Australia has one of the strongest consumer protection laws globally to stop people (individuals and corporations) from exploiting vulnerable users. These protections include prohibiting people from making misleading or deceptive statements, ensuring the goods or services are of merchantable quality and fit for the intended purpose, and preventing unconscionable conduct. While these provisions apply broadly to every transaction, they are particularly important in the provision of new products or services, such as a blockchain loyalty program, where the user may not have any prior experience or knowledge and the product may not be fully developed and tested at the time of the transaction.

The relevant sections in the Australian Consumer Law (**ACL**) are:

- Misleading or deceptive conduct - 'a person must not, in trade or commerce, engage in conduct that is misleading or deceptive or is likely to mislead or deceive' (s.18 ACL)

- False or misleading representations about goods or services: as to the value, standard or quality of goods, or that the person making the representation has a sponsorship, approval or affiliation; or with respect to the price of the goods and services.(s.29(1)(a))

- Unconscionable conduct in connection with goods and services (s.21)

- Misleading representations with respect to future matters: if the person does not have reasonable grounds for making the representation it will be taken to be misleading. (s.4)

The above provisions were sculpted to reflect that of the Consumer Protection from Unfair Trading Regulations in the United Kingdom, which provides a general ban on conduct below a level which harm, or are likely to harm the economic interests of the average consumer. It is worth noting that, in Australia, the Australian Competition and Consumer Commission's jurisdiction around Initial Coin Offerings and the ACL has been delegated to ASIC, permitting ASIC to exercise jurisdiction around token offerings where there is a concern that a breach of the ACL has occurred. Australia is considered to have very pro-consumer laws, and the regulatory framework provides a useful guide for loyalty program operators to consider their system design as well as terms and conditions of the program.

5. Unfair contracts

Generally, Australian contract law has endeavoured to follow in the footsteps of jurisdictions around the world in their response terms which can be considered by a Court or Tribunal to be unfair contract terms. Legislation such as the *Unfair Contract Terms Act* 1977 in the United Kingdom, and the European Commission Unfair Contract terms directive, have used notion of "good faith" to regulate imbalances between the rights and obligations of the consumer, and that of the sellers and suppliers. In America, the threshold to determine whether a contract term is unfair is significantly higher, as a term will only be unfair if it can shown to be 'unconscionable', which means that a term is so terribly unfair that the contract simply cannot be allowed to stand as is.

Accordingly, in Australia, enforcement bodies such as the ACCC and NSW Fair Trading have moulded their approach to regulating unfair contract terms in a similar vein to that of the above countries, primarily the United Kingdom. In particular, the ACCC has prioritised ensuring consumer contracts are fair and transparent regarding the rights of both parties involved. In recent years, the ACCC have emphasised their focus on holding both big and small businesses accountable for knowingly inserting unfair contract terms, and stepped up enforcement against businesses to ensure that their standard contracts do not contain such terms. Key provisions within the ACL are examples of such incentives.

Part 2-3 of the ACL, set out in Schedule 2 to the *Competition and Consumer Act 2010* (Cth) (**CCA**) contains the first Australia-wide prohibition of unfair contract terms, in certain circumstances. Part 2-3 of chapter 2 of the ACL renders a contract term void if:

- the contract in question is a 'consumer contract'; and
- the contract in question is a 'standard form contract'; and
- the impugned contract term is unfair.

First of all, a consumer contract is a contract for the supply of goods or services to an individual consumer, who buys the good or service wholly or predominantly for personal, domestic or household use or consumption. Section 23(1)(b) of the ACL confines the prohibition of unfair contract terms to those in a 'standard form contract', which is defined as a contract that is pre-prepared for its customers, and not open to negotiation by the consumer. In accordance with section 24 of the ACL, a term of a standard form consumer contract is unfair if; it would cause a significant imbalance in the rights and obligations of the parties under the contract, it is not reasonably necessary to protect the legitimate interests of the party advantaged by the term, or it would cause detriment to a party if it is applied or relied on. Section 25 of the ACL goes on to set out various examples of contract terms which may be unfair.

To the extent that tokens within a blockchain loyalty scheme are considered a good being provided wholly or predominantly to the requisite users for personal or domestic use, the unfair contracts regime will apply. Accordingly, if any pre-sale of loyalty tokens fail to meet the test of transparency pursuant to s 24(3) of the CCA, and are subsequently challenged and found to be unfair, they can be rendered void, and therefore not form part of the agreement including whether or not they are embodied in a smart contract. As such, terms that may be declared unfair within the commencement of any pre-sale, and limit the company's liability or obligations under the token loyalty scheme, are of the kind which the ACCC and the ACL identify as terms which:

- permits one party, but not another party, to avoid or limit its performance of its obligations under the contract

- penalises one party, but not the other party, for a breach or termination of the contract

- permits one party, but not another party, to terminate, vary or renew the contract

- permits one party to vary the upfront price under the contract without the right of the other party to terminate the contract

Further, a court may decide that a particular term is unfair, if the court determines that the clause leads to a significant imbalance in the parties rights and obligations, or is not reasonably necessary to protect the legitimate interests of the party who benefits from the term in the context of the whole agreement. On 12 November 2016, there were significant amendments introduced to the unfair contract term provisions of the ACL, extending the operation of the unfair contract terms regime to small businesses. A small business is defined as a business who employ fewer than 20 employees. Since the amendments were introduced, the ACCC has demonstrated that it is willing to litigate to enforce the unfair contract provisions of the ACL.

Notably, one of the first enforcement actions taken by the ACCC was against JJ Richard in the case of *ACCC v JJ Richards & Sons Pty Ltd* (2017), where the ACCC alleged that JJ Richard's standard form contract contained eight unfair contract terms. The offending terms included clauses which purported to; bind customers to commit to subsequent contracts unless they cancel the contract within 30 days, allowing JJ Richards to unilaterally increase its prices, and remove any liability where its performance is "prevented or hindered in any way." Following the *JJ Richards* case, a host of other firms were investigated, including; *Servcorp,* where it was held that businesses can no longer impose contract terms that create a significant power imbalance between parties; *Equifax,* whereby the ACCC alleged that Equifax's renewal term for its credit report service was deemed void under the ACL, and *Cardronics,* where several unfair terms including an automatic renewal and a unilateral increase of fees were all deemed void and invalid.

Although the above cases reinforce the ACCC's investigative powers in identifying unfair contract terms, it must be noted however, that the unfairness of each term is evaluated upon the circumstances of the usage of the term. As such, it cannot be guaranteed at this stage, that the ACL offers a requisite barrier to the inclusion of such terms in consumer contracts.

Critically, at this stage the ACL does not provide for penalties for breaches of the unfair contract provisions. If a term is determined by a court to be an unenforceable unfair contract term, then the clause is merely voided. There is no mechanism for the party which imposed the unfair term to be penalised. Historically, the ACCC has merely accepted court-enforceable undertakings to amend offending contracts to remove unfair terms. However, there are currently proposals before the federal Government to amend the ACL to allow the ACCC to seek civil financial penalties when a contract term is declared unfair and void. It remains to be seen whether these proposals will come to be incorporated into the ACL.

6. Future developments

The use of blockchain technology is constantly evolving and developing and the law will always be catching up. Smart contracts offer great automation and efficiency but are still largely untested in the courts and unregulated, but as can be seen throughout this chapter, various existing regulatory systems interact with loyalty schemes using blockchain.

As such, the design and operation of any loyalty scheme should take place with considered legal advice, and a blockchain loyalty scheme is no different, but needs additional care at the earliest stages to manage the new risks that come with this new technology.

CHAPTER 9

BLOCKCHAIN GAMIFICATION

Gamification is the use of elements of gameplay in non-game contexts to stimulate specific behaviours. Gamification can play a key role in loyalty and reward programs because it has the potential to make a mundane task less boring and can motivate members to engage in very specific, desirable behaviours.

It is important to explore gamification within the context of blockchain loyalty for three reasons. Firstly, blockchain companies have actively used gamification techniques during ICOs and post ICOs to build communities and generate investment. Secondly, cryptocurrencies and cryptotokens have the potential to inject significant value into mainstream gamification approaches, and as we know from our analysis in Chapter 4, value is a major contributor to member engagement. Thirdly, there are a small number of blockchain companies who have led with gamification as their core customer experience.

Gamification delivers a range of useful tools to facilitate engagement, including points, badges, levels, leaderboards and challenges. Google's Local Guides program is a wonderful example of the application of these tools to motivate a very specific behaviour. Local Guides was designed to generate massive amounts of business related content for Search and Google Maps, thereby enabling users to easily access lots of individual opinions and photos related to a business they may be considering visiting. Local Guides members all around the world earn points for different activities, including:

- Writing a review: 5 points per review.
- Providing a rating: 1 point per rating.

- Submitting a photo: 5 points per photo.

- Answering a question (e.g. is there wheelchair access?): 1 point per answer.

- Editing incorrect details: 5 points per edit.

- Adding a new place: 15 points per place added.

- Checking facts (e.g. opening times): 1 point per fact checked.

The points add up to unlock up to ten levels and seven badges, which provide different benefits to members:

- Level 1 (0 points): monthly newsletter, access to Google hosted workshops and Hangouts, and (in select countries) exclusive contests.

- Level 2 (15 points): early access to new Google products and features, option to promote your own meet-ups on the Local Guides calendar.

- Level 3 (75 points): a Local Guides badge in Google Maps, the option to connect with other Local Guides via an exclusive Google+ community, option to moderate Local Guides community channels and invites to Google hosted events in selected cities.

- Level 4 (250 points): badge, plus free Google Drive storage upgrade of 100GB and option to be featured in Local Guides online channels.

- Level 5 (500 points): badge, plus get to be a Google insider, testing new products before public release.

- Level 6 (1,500 points): badge plus ad hoc benefits.

- Level 7 (5,000 points): badge plus ad hoc benefits.

- Level 8 (15,000 points): badge plus ad hoc benefits.

- Level 9 (50,000 points): badge plus ad hoc benefits.

- Level 10 (100,000 points): badge plus ad hoc benefits.

Any reviews posted by the member show their profile, which includes their level and their badge. To keep the engagement going, Google released four new badges in November 2017: Reviewer, Photographer, Trailblazer and Fact Finder.

Higher level tiers also have the option to apply to attend the annual, all expenses paid Local Guides summit, an annual conference where Google hosts the most engaged Local Guides from around the world.

An interesting element of the program is Google Communities. Local Guides allows reviewers to host meet ups, where they can invite other local reviewers to get together and explore the neighbourhood, then post their experience onto Google Maps. Examples on the website include San Francisco (the group mapped an interesting walking path through the city and photographed the whole thing), London (the group mapped out a route of the cafes with the best coffee) and New York (the group mapped out the city's finest ramen joints).

Local Guides also uses challenges as part of the program. In July 2017, they invited members to celebrate local restaurants by sharing photos of them on Google Maps. Members were asked to show off their photos on social media using the specific hashtags, #LocalGuides and #OnGoogleMaps, for the chance to be featured on the Local Guide channels.

Local Guides has been enormously successful in generating masses of useful, quality content for Google products at a tiny cost to their business. Google has a fantastic opportunity to stick their toe in the crypto pool with Local Guides. By creating a cryptotoken specifically for members and rewarding them for quality posts they would inject a significant amount of value into the program and turbo-charge engagement at scale. They could quickly extend the token usage to a loyalty program across global retailers, where members can earn the token for transacting at participating retailers and in a short period of time create the world's biggest and most valuable loyalty program.

The most widely applied model for gamification theory is the Fogg Behavior Model.[25] The creator, B.J. Fogg, is a Stanford University professor who proposed that three elements (motivation, ability and trigger) must converge at the same moment for a behaviour to occur.

---

25 http://www.behaviormodel.org/

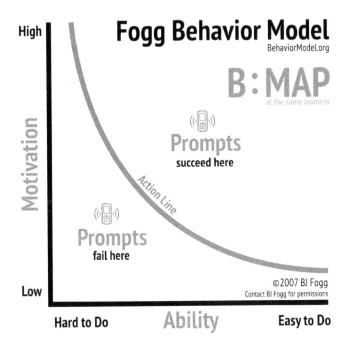

To illustrate, if a blockchain company wishes for their community members to promote their upcoming ICO, Fogg's model can provide them with guidance on how to stimulate the base. Specifically:

- Motivation: the key motivation of the community is their desire to earn cryptotokens.

- Ability: most members of the community will have the ability to promote the ICO via social media channels.

- Trigger: the blockchain company can provide them with free cryptotokens for completing set tasks.

This scenario is playing out across ICOs and social media on a daily basis. Zeepin ICO rewarded community members with free ZPT tokens for following them on social media, sharing articles on Facebook, Twitter and Telegram, as well as translating articles into different languages and even writing press releases, making it a very well publicised capital raising.

Companies such as Earn.com (which will be discussed more extensively

---

26 Reproduced with permission Professor B.J. Fogg

in Chapter 15), reward members with free cryptotoken airdrops for following promoted blockchain companies on Telegram and other tasks.

Fogg also details different trigger types which are based on the degree of the member's motivation and ability. Someone with a high motivation but low ability requires a *facilitator* trigger, where they are provided with support, such as basic education. Someone with a high motivation and ability may require a *signal* trigger, which could be as simple as blowing a whistle to tell them they can start. Someone with low motivation but high ability may require a *spark* trigger, such as the promise of additional bonus benefits to light their fire. From a gamification perspective, understanding the motivation and ability levels of the member base is critical to the success of the campaign.

Here's some further examples of companies adopting blockchain gamification approaches:

HotNow

www.hotoken.io

One big opportunity for gamification within blockchain loyalty is a campaign where the entire ecosystem is rewarded with cryptotokens to stimulate the organic expansion of a large, engaged community. This can lead to a virtuous cycle, where each task generates a positive benefit, which facilitates the manifestation of the next task and benefit. In this situation, the growth of the community drives greater demand for the cryptotokens, increasing its value and generating more demand.

An example of a company utilising this gamification approach is HotNow and their Hotoken value system. HotNow rewards its participants with Hotoken for every action completed which contributes to the growth of the ecosystem. For example, referrals which lead to new users becoming active on the platform, buying and selling products and services, participating in social activities and writing reviews. Consumers can utilise Hotoken to gain access to retailers deals and promotions advertised on HotNow, while retailers can use Hotoken to bid for exposure and pay for targeted advertising and other related services.

Similar to Google's Local Guides, members can earn Hotoken for identifying good retailers and providing ratings. HotNow also offers a portfolio of casual games in the HotNow app which are designed to expand the range of marketing opportunities for retailers. The games have embedded marketing messaging in them and by playing, members have the chance to win Hotoken. Thus, retailers can reward members with Hotoken which can be used at retailers, generating continual demand and a community centred around a desire to earn more and more of a finite cryptotoken.

Steem

www.steem.com

Steem is a social blockchain company that grows communities and makes revenue streams possible for users by rewarding them for creating and sharing content. It powers social app Steemit, which pays content creators in Steem cryptotokens when their work receives votes. People who vote for the content are rewarded for helping to curate the best content available on the site and those who write comments are rewarded also. Content creators can get started by creating a free account and submitting an article, then waiting for those precious votes to roll in. The approach effectively rewards everyone for participation, with content writing, reading and commenting becoming an intellectual game on a global community level.

Launching at around US 65 cents, Steem peaked during the 2017-2018 bull market at US$7.31 before dropping to a low of 28 cents in early-2019.

Peerguess

www.peerguess.com

One company has gamified the process of predicting cryptocurrency and token future valuations. Peerguess offers an app which allows members to create a portfolio of cryptocurrencies and tokens to monitor. They can then select one of these currencies and make a gamified prediction on the direction of price. New members are gifted one hundred GEMS, the cryptotoken central to the program. Within the app, they can select GEMS to wager on the price direction of a particular currency within their portfolio, either up or down. For example, they could bet that the price of Ether will go up in the next 24 hours. If their prediction turns out to be correct, they double their bet, but if incorrect, the GEMS are lost. Fortunately, there's some compassion from the Peerguess team. If a member loses all their GEMS, they automatically receive an additional ten into their account, so they can stay in the game. With the right level of involvement, Peerguess aims to evolve into a community app with genuine predictive powers, which will prove a very valuable thing for investors and a novel application of gamification theory.

Pigzbe

www.pigzbe.com

Pigzbe is designed to help teach children the principles of modern finance using a blockchain gamification approach. It's a digital piggy-wallet for children aged 6 and up, powered by the Wollo cryptotoken.

The whitepaper describes Pigzbe as 'a friendly, tangible financial assistant that will teach children the principles of modern money in an exciting and safe system that harnesses children's natural drive to learn through self-correcting, practical experimentation… Think of Pigzbe as a tool to support parents in teaching children the principles of earning, saving and managing money in an exciting and non-threatening way, while providing them with an entry point into the world of cryptocurrencies.'

Although there are 2.2 billion children in the world, Pigzbe sees their target market as the 205 million children who get up to $15 pocket money each week.

Pigzbe delivers a combination of software and hardware which includes:

- Wollo (WLO): The Pigzbe network's native token, replacing money stored in piggy banks.

- Wallet app & educational game: Allows for the transfer of pocket money to children safely, quickly, and cost effectively with an app for parents and a game for children that enables the learning and playing experience.

- Game controller & cold storage device: Kids can use the Pigzbe Pink device as a notifier and controller for the Pigzbe game. Adults can use Pigzbe Black as a secure cold storage device to keep their Wollo safe.

- Wollo Card, for real world spending: Through a partnership with Wirex, Pigzbe have developed a payment card that will allow children and families to spend Wollo in multiple currencies, online and offline, in the real world.

Once registered for Pigzbe, children can receive Wollo from their parents (including recurring allowances and gifts), play and learn with the Pigzbe game and achieve goals set by their parents.

In November 2018, Pigzbe completed a US$8.8 million ICO, an impressive achievement given its timing in the bear market. They also won the right to have their Wollo token listed on Bitfinex at no cost to the Pigzbe team after they won the ICO Race held in Lugano in June 2018. To cap off their stellar year, the team also managed to negotiate the partnership with Wirex. Wirex are the only company in Europe with a debit card that is linked to users' crypto wallets, allowing them to convert crypto and spend in over 40 million retailers. This would appear to be the perfect partnership for Pigzbe as it will allow children to earn Wollo as pocket money through the app and spend it anywhere. Pigzbe is well positioned to deliver on their core mission of educating the future generation about financial literacy in a truly cashless and borderless financial system.

Financial literacy is being viewed as an increasingly important area and one which is on the UN's radar. Companies like Pigzbe are using blockchain gamification techniques to make learning about a dry subject lots of fun for both children and parents.

CHAPTER 10
RUNNING A CRYPTOTOKEN ICO

To DATE, MOST blockchain loyalty companies have engaged in Initial Coin Offerings (or Initial Token Offers (ITO)) to raise essential seed funding to establish their blockchain loyalty program. Running an ICO also serves the purpose of injecting cryptotokens into the investment community to trade on exchanges, which builds a market price and a market for the cryptotoken when loyalty earn behaviour commences.

It is important to note that an ICO is not an essential step for launching a blockchain loyalty program. As a loyalty management consultant, I recommend against it. A company that doesn't have capital-raising requirements would be much better off creating a cryptotoken, launching it on an exchange, then conducting an airdrop to their community and relevant crypto investors to generate trading behaviour (as per Japanese company Line). This also includes established loyalty programs which aim to convert their points or miles into a cryptotoken. The key advantage of this approach (outside of avoiding the need to run an ICO) is better control over the token supply, as the company only needs to release enough tokens into the community to stimulate trading behaviour.

Most companies to date have taken the ICO route however the opportunity to collect enough seed-funding for the first 2-3 years of operation without having to relinquish any equity in the business has been considered too good an opportunity to pass up. Based on that, this chapter provides a general introduction to organising and running an ICO.

The best way to think about an ICO is as a more sophisticated crowdfunding program. Crowdfunding platforms such as Kickstarter, GoFundMe and Indiegogo continue to be very successful models for supporting start-ups to raise essential seed funding but they also have some limitations. Once the funding has been provided to the start-up, the funder has no control over it and no sense of potential returned value, other than early access to the product or service or a discount. If they wish to liquidate their investment, it is very difficult or impossible.

With an ICO, the investor is provided with something specific for their investment; cryptotokens. While a cryptotoken is not a share of the business ownership, it can sometimes carry with it the promise of a return. (For example, *trade.io* conducted an ICO where holders of their TIO tokens earn a share of profits generated as a "security token"). More importantly, the investor is provided with something relatively liquid in exchange for their funds, which they can sell on a digital exchange if they no longer wish to maintain their holding.

ICOs came out of nowhere and the rules on how to run one are still being written. The following approach is a basic overview but it is important to remember there are many variations on this structure. Each ICO is different and needs to be designed with the specific requirements of the business in mind. It is recommended to consider hiring the services of an ICO advisory agency, particularly one which has a track record of running successful ICOs, as they will be able to provide clear guidance on the optimal approach.

The first step to run a decent sized ICO is securing seed funding. It can cost anywhere from US$250,000 to US$500,000 to run, with most of the costs going to marketing and staff. Not surprisingly, an ICO is a marketing exercise. Likely potential investors will request an advanced version of a whitepaper, plus a detailed overview of the company vision, financial structure, team and other elements.

The whitepaper clearly defines the vision for the company, as well as the structure of the ICO and the terms and conditions. It is worth spending some moments reading and researching both blockchain loyalty and non-loyalty whitepapers to get a sense of their structure and approach, and to obtain clear direction. The whitepaper is an essential document which allows the company to briefly outline the technical features of the system under development, thus appealing to both experts and a wider community of enthusiasts and early adopters. Whitepapers are generally not overly promotional but are aimed at experts and opinion leaders who wish to better learn about the technical elements of the product. One vital section of the whitepaper is the roadmap, which will provide clear details on when the product or service will launch, how it will be developed and evolved using the ICO funding and how it will change the world. It is also useful to create a simplified, essentialised version of the whitepaper to present the core offering in a few pages.

A feasibility assessment is required to ensure the business and ICO approach will be compliant with legal and regulatory requirements. This can be challenging in the rapidly changing world of blockchain as governments worldwide scramble to make sense of it and either overreact— banning cryptocurrencies outright— or open up the market with tax-free crypto trading policies.

Suffice to say, the assessment should be focussed on the country in which the business will be based, while considering other countries which could cause future issues. This includes the US, with its restrictions on securities trading. Because the regulatory landscape is uncertain, a good lawyer will not only consider the current requirements but also research and anticipate the future requirements to ensure the business is protected from any legislative evolution. Having a reputable law firm and accounting firm conduct the feasibility is wise for two reasons. Firstly, the business can take confidence in knowing the best people will be working on the assessment to protect against current and future regulatory requirements. Secondly, the names of the assessors can be quoted on the website to raise the confidence of potential investors that the ICO is legitimate and the business trustworthy. The main downside is the cost involved in accessing these firms. The business needs to consider a balance of brand name firms and budget management.

It is also worthwhile considering using the services of an ICO rating agency such as ICORating, ICObench or Hacked. These companies review the ICO and provide a rating across a range of measures, including profile, team, vision and product. The rating agencies can provide valuable promotional support by featuring the ICO on their website which is a place many potential investors will look for opportunities. A high rating can play a critical role in securing community support for the ICO.

With the completion of feasibility, the team can turn to the preparation phase. This involves completing the whitepaper, developing a detailed campaign plan, building the website, creating content, registering social media accounts, building a PR strategy, booking roadshows, hiring the promotional team and setting an ICO target date. It is key during this phase to develop a community of supporters and potential investors which can be used to recruit a wider community with a multiplier effect, such that when the ICO opens, the support is established and the next phase happens quickly and effortlessly.

The campaign plan should involve a combination of targeting high-end investors and mass market investors. Targeting people who haven't invested in cryptocurrencies or tokens before is not advised because it will require a great deal of effort to explain to them the process required to register for an exchange, create a crypto wallet, purchase a major cryptocurrency (such as Bitcoin or Ether) to invest, complete the KYC/AML processes and all the other intricacies involved. The downside is the business is chasing the same group of investors who are also being chased by every other ICO run at the same time, making it a very competitive process. This means a well-coordinated digital and traditional marketing approach is key for success. Ideally, the plan will utilise all the latest digital promotional approaches to reach the right audience, including pay per click (PPC), display and banner advertising plus email marketing, SEO and content marketing strategies, as well as gamification approaches. ICO and cryptocurrency advertising bans implemented by Google[27], Facebook[28] and Twitter[29] in 2018 made this exceptionally challenging.

The ICO website is the main promotional vehicle and needs to be exceptionally well designed. Ideally, it will contain an overview of the problem being solved by the company and the proposed solution, a summary of the cryptocurrency and the role it plays in the ecosystem, the ambition of the company, an overview of the team and advisors, details for the ICO approach, any ICO ratings which have been ascertained by professional rating agencies, links to any press articles, details of any proof of work executions demonstrating the technology being funded, the development roadmap, a well maintained blog,

---

27 https://www.coindesk.com/google-to-ban-cryptocurrency-ico-ads-from-june/
28 https://techcrunch.com/2018/01/30/
facebook-is-banning-cryptocurrency-and-ico-ads/
29 https://www.coindesk.com/twitter-will-ban-crypto-ads-starting-tomorrow/

FAQ, contact options and the ability for a potential investor to easily create an investment account so they can participate by transferring in funds. It is also useful to access suitable direct denial of service (DDoS) protection software, such as Cloudflare. Anyone visiting the website should immediately be able to understand what the company's vision is and why society absolutely needs the service on blockchain. If they cannot comprehend that in a few seconds, the core marketing message requires revision. It is recommended to create at least one video to provide a straight-forward overview of the company's vision and inspire potential investors to immediately sign up to the whitelist.

One of the key drivers of engagement with a company running an ICO is good quality content. Whitepapers are generally quite complex technical documents and it will only be a minority of investors who actually take the time to read completely, if at all. The role content marketing can play is to introduce the vision and potential of the company in a digestible way, allowing for mass penetration of the key messages and leading to engagement with a large supporter base. Developing good quality content isn't easy, therefore this stage of the process is useful to get an early start. The marketing campaign plan will detail all the different channels which will require content. The content developer can map the relevant style of content design for the specific channels. They can then begin the content creation process. When the execution phase begins, legally compliant, well-crafted content will already be prepared and released as required.

Social media and messaging applications are by far the most powerful channel an ICO marketing team has at their disposal to build the required community of supporters. Most ICOs utilise multiple channels including Facebook, Twitter, LinkedIn, YouTube, Vimeo, Telegram, Instagram, Medium, WeChat, WhatsApp, Reddit, GitHub, Youku, Steemit and Sina Weibo. Further support is provided by email, chatbots and live chat. Because of the importance of these channels, it is necessary to allocate the right level of resources to support them, including 24 hour support for the main channels. Off the back of this, companies like OmniSparx have developed solutions which allow the management of all communication channels through a single platform, including the ability to reward individuals with cryptocurrency allocations. Some ICOs nominate a primary channel, such as Telegram, and recommend it as the preferred option for supporter communications to consolidate discussions. It is not unusual for passionate supporters to take on a de facto role of an administrator and attempt to answer the questions of those looking for support. An important social media event in the lead-up to an ICO is an 'ask me anything' event, where the leaders of the business invite potential investors to post questions for live responses, which provides interested parties with a great deal of confidence, particularly if the leaders can deliver solid responses to difficult questions or challenges to their approach. At the very least, direct contact with the public shows the leadership team themselves are prepared to get out there and converse, indicating they believe in what they're doing.

The PR strategy can follow a traditional PR approach, as well as take advantage of new media channels including CoinDesk, Cointelegraph and Bitcoin Talk. It is essential to be prepared, ensuring the business is ready to provide media organisations with the core, essential information required to generate a story. It is also worthwhile investing in media training for spokespeople.

Roadshows play an important role in attracting major investors. It is not unusual for a pre ICO to be completely dominated by a small number of large investors, which is beneficial to the business, as it provides an important injection of early funding which can be reinvested in marketing activity to stimulate engagement with the main ICO. Roadshows can be independent or tied to regular, international blockchain conferences. The roadshow should be headed up by the company CEO, although a prominent advisor associated with the ICO can also be extremely useful. A roadshow presentation can quickly evolve into a negotiation with a major investor seeking better terms for their investment, therefore the company representative should be prepared to engage as required.

The operational team required for a reasonably sized ICO will grow to around 10 to 14 people. Required resources include a campaign manager, PPC manager, email marketing manager, website manager, bounty manager and a small team of community managers, supported by an operations manager, content manager, legal resource and ICO lead. The team will be expected to work long and challenging hours during the execution phase and need to be able to perform in a coordinated manner. The team with the most pressure are the community managers, who will be required to work shifts, and will grow weary of answering the same basic questions day after day by potential investors who have not taken the time to seek the easily available answers from the FAQ's on the website.

Aside from the ICO marketing team, the business needs to construct the main operational team. It is important that the team carry solid credentials which provide potential investors with confidence that the project is in good hands. If required, credentials can also be boosted by accessing the services of professional advisors. For example, the NAGA ICO, which raised $57 million included the advisory services of Roger Ver (Founder and CEO, Bitcoin.com), Mate Tokay (COO, Bitcoin.com), Miko Matsumura (Cofounder, Evercoin) and Guy Ben-Artzi (Cofounder, Bancor); a heavy-weight team. Transparency is essential, which means photos, names, titles and links to LinkedIn profiles are vital, so potential investors can easily research those involved and determine their experience and suitability for executing the project.

The next phase is execution. The ICO marketing team should now be fully up to speed, such that when the ICO is announced, the machine can kick into gear. This phase involves starting the marketing activity, conducting A/B testing of the website to optimise the layout and content, starting email marketing, commencing bounty marketing and gamification, getting roadshows underway, disseminating content via the new social media accounts to begin building the community and ideally engaging big investors in negotiations to lock in critical early funding.

The most exciting part of the execution phase from a loyalty perspective is the bounty marketing and gamification. ICOs provide an enormous opportunity to utilise the community to build the community. Some of the clever approaches used by ICOs include rewarding community members with small amounts of the new cryptotokens for registering for the whitelist, connecting via social media channels, inviting others to invest (using a unique link to track), creating and sharing memes, answering quizzes and writing blog or social media content. Tapping into the community is an incredibly cost effective way to generate maximum exposure, particularly when they're rewarded with the new cryptotokens, which cost nothing to create. It also has the added benefit of spreading the cryptotokens to a wider base, which is important when talking with exchanges who favour large community groups.

It's vital not to neglect a crisis management plan. Things can (and do) go wrong with ICOs, therefore having a clear recovery approach is critical to get things back on track in a timely manner. Some of the main crises related to ICOs include scammers providing potential investors with the wrong wallet address via fake websites and emails to steal their currency, websites not being able to cope with the traffic and crashing, hackers attacking the website itself, DDoS attacks, an understaffed community team not being able to cope with a tidal wave of last minute inquiries plus many more scenarios. Often crises are unavoidable but what is possible is having a clear action plan so if something does go wrong the team knows exactly how to react in a strategic and effective manner.

One crucial communication task is to inform potential investors to not transfer their cryptocurrency investment in the ICO from an exchange. There are a few reasons for this. Firstly, exchanges don't always process their withdrawals immediately. They may batch them or there may be heavy traffic on the site which creates processing delays. They also don't allow users to set their gas (the transaction fee paid for a cryptocurrency transfer), meaning further delays if there's heavy traffic on the blockchain platform. I have experienced delays of up to five days when transferring cryptocurrencies and tokens from an exchange into my private wallet. Secondly, the ICOs are generally structured so the coins are sent to the same address from where the deposit was made. If this is an exchange address, the coins can easily get lost, especially if the exchange doesn't support the new currency. Thirdly, the company running the ICO needs to be able to tie the incoming deposit to an account. It is common for the company to request a personal wallet address as part of the registration process but if the deposit comes from a different address, such as an exchange, reconciling the transaction to the account isn't possible without intervention.

There are a large number of digital trading exchanges and during the execution phase it will be necessary to engage some of them to persuade them to range the new cryptocurrency. This can often involve paying a substantial fee, as well as passing some significant due diligence criteria. Some exchanges, such as KuCoin, create shortlists of potential coins then invite their members to vote on which one they should range (which includes charging a voting fee in KCS, KuCoin's own cryptotoken). With a large number of ICOs and new cryptocurrencies being created every day, competition for exchange listings is intense, with businesses aware that landing their coin on a major exchange can dramatically increase their exposure. One thing which is common to all exchanges is the need for a reasonable number of cryptotoken holders. Even if the ICO has eventuated in a small number of major investors, there will be little interest from exchanges to proceed with a listing, as they seek volume of trades to support their business model. A cryptocurrency which isn't traded often, due to a concentration of ownership by a few, is of no interest to them. Thus, bounty marketing and gamification can play an early role in building this essential spread of ownership, while simultaneously building engagement and interest in the ICO.

When planning an ICO or the creation of a cryptocurrency or token it is prudent to communicate a number of key risks to potential investors within the ICO documentation.

Today, almost every company in the world is dependent on computer technology to function which is vulnerable to outages caused by a range of issues including (but not limited to) viruses and hacks. It is critical to advise investors that the company cannot provide assurances that a system failure would not adversely affect the use of the cryptotoken.

Blockchain technology is very new, as are smart contracts and there may be unrecognised flaws in the structure which could lead to technical problems and the inability for an investor to access or utilise their cryptotokens. Investors should be made aware that there is risk involved by utilising this new technology.

The rapid evolution of blockchain technology means that most governments are dizzy with the pace of it. Few countries have yet to establish reasonable regulatory guidelines regarding the use of blockchain technology and cryptocurrencies, particularly for blockchain loyalty programs, although existing legal and tax regulation does cover a great deal as we have seen. There is much nervousness and panic amongst some governments and central banks regarding the large amounts of money some people are investing. There are fears that it could suddenly ruin the financial future of millions of people. As new regulations come into place, it could mean that the laws conflict with the setup of the smart contract and/or the cryptotoken. This may mean that the company is no longer able to offer services within the specific country or they must change their service offering, which could have severe negative implications on the valuation of their business.

Most blockchain companies are already actively avoiding potential regulatory hotspots. For example, the Giftz ICO for itCoin Black included in their terms, 'Governments are still grappling with public policy on the regulation of cryptocurrencies as a form of settlement in trade. Governments adverse to the proliferation of the use of cryptocurrencies in local commerce could issue laws and regulations deeming the use of cryptocurrencies a regulated activity. In recent weeks, countries such as China and Korea have issued regulations or statements prohibiting token sales, while other countries have sought to bring the sale of tokens within the regulator control of securities offerings. This could result in holders of itCoin Blacks being unable to use their itCoin Blacks in the future without further regulatory compliance by itCoin Black.'

The NAGA ICO whitepaper was even more specific. 'You are not eligible and not allowed to participate in the NAGA ICO (as referred to in this Whitepaper) as well as in the Token Sale Referral Program, if you are a citizen, resident (tax or otherwise) or green card holder of the United States of America, People's Republic of China or a citizen or resident of the Republic of Singapore, Socialist Republic of Vietnam or resident of a country where American embargoes and sanctions are in force, namely Iran, North Korea, Syria, Sudan, or Cuba.'

Different countries have different tax rules regarding cryptocurrency and token ownership and trading. As mentioned earlier, some countries, such as Belarus, have declared no taxes are payable on profits generated from crypto trading, while others, such as the US, have stated that each trade is a taxable event. Investors need to be made aware that taxes may be payable on any profits they may make from the ICO and it is their responsibility to comply with those laws relevant to their jurisdiction. Just as variations in tax laws across companies have been exploited by companies seeking to minimise their tax obligations, leading to the offshoring of business units and capital, it is likely that cryptocurrencies and cryptotokens will follow a similar flow, as wealthy investors seek tax friendly havens.

When cryptocurrencies emerged, the owners could act completely anonymously. Even now, there are Bitcoin owners holding reserves totalling tens of millions of dollars with nothing to tie them to that ownership. One of the main regulatory steps governments around the world are taking is forcing trading exchanges and blockchain businesses to adopt proper AML/CTF processes. This will then enable government agencies to access the trading history of individuals to combat tax avoidance, money laundering, drug trafficking and other illegal activities. Investors need to be made aware that their personal details may be provided to law enforcement, government officials and other third parties if required.

In the perfect world, an investor would buy a cryptocurrency or token, or a loyalty program member would earn a cryptotoken, and the value would gradually but consistently increase over time. In reality, it is likely the value will fluctuate, possibly wildly. As the free market has the majority control over the value of the tokens after they've been floated on an exchange, investors need to be aware that they may suffer a loss if the currency value decreases. Even with participatory commitment from retail partners and extensive expertise within the team to execute a high-quality program, there is no guarantee that the company will dramatically increase the value of the currency. In addition, investors need to be aware that they may not be able to access the cryptotokens. For example, the tokens could be listed on a single exchange which they're unable to access. It's also possible that they may not be able to sell their holding when they wish, for similar reasons.

If the ICO doesn't go according to plan, there's a risk that the company may not achieve their capital raising target. This may be due to a poor marketing plan, a lack of interest in their vision, concerns over the quality of the team or a variety of other reasons outside the control of management. In that instance, the investor may be left holding a cryptotoken which doesn't have sufficient liquidity to generate meaningful trading activity. It may also require the company to completely restructure their business strategy. The company needs to advise potential investors of these risks and make them aware they have little recourse if the development roadmap detailed in the whitepaper is no longer achievable due to the lack of funds raised.

Investors needs to be informed that purchasing the cryptocurrency does not constitute any ownership of the company; quite a different scenario to purchasing shares for a publicly listed company.

With everything in place plus a large, engaged community of willing investors, it is time for the ICO to commence. An ICO can be a single event or it may be several events. The EZToken ICO was run in four stages: a pre ICO which was restricted to retailers and provided a 50 per cent discount, followed by three further rounds, each with reduced discounts per round but larger token allocations. Running the ICO in stages allows for an early injection of funding, which can be reinvested in marketing for the main event, as well as creating a fear of missing out (FOMO) due to the restriction in tokens available. One advisor suggested the ideal ICO round should take no more than three days, with 80 per cent of the funds received in the first day. There are numerous ICOs which run for weeks or months, costing large amounts in marketing funds and reducing the confidence of early investors in the company's ability to hit their hard cap funding target. A better approach is a long lead up period with extensive community building activities, followed by a rapid sale to a mass market audience, ideally leaving behind lots of unmet demand which will feed into strong take up when the currency is floated on an exchange.

With the sale completed, funds need to be audited and accounts synchronised. Despite best communication efforts to remind participants not to transfer their investment directly from an exchange, a percentage of investors will do this anyway, requiring manual processing of payments to ensure tokens are allocated correctly. (These same investors will soak up a healthy amount of attention from the community team). Once the reconciliation and audit are completed, the tokens need to be distributed to the investors. With the majority of the financiers investing with major cryptocurrencies instead of cash, it is important to convert everything to fiat as quickly as possible to ensure the value of the holding isn't significantly diminished by a sudden drop in the market. Conversations with exchanges need to ramp up quickly to secure a listing, as the new investors will be eager to discover the market value of what they've just purchased and even more eager to start trading. Through an extensive social media effort in the lead up to the ICO, the interaction will grow as investor and potential new investors seek information about the company and assurances that the value of their new holding is going to grow. Some investors, particularly major investors, will require more attention than others. There will also be a need for clear governance of the company to ensure the coin reserves and the ICO funds are managed appropriately.

With ICO funds successfully deposited into the company's bank account, the real work starts; developing the loyalty platform, hiring the team, building the retailer network, planning the launch marketing campaigns, designing the app and every other task required to run a world class blockchain loyalty program.

Hopefully there will be at least one night for the team to drink a few glasses of Taittinger.

As ICO approaches evolve rapidly, a trend which became mainstream in mid-2018 involved most or all of the cryptotoken allocation being secured by large investors in the private ICO stage. One advantage for the blockchain company is that concentrating the cryptotokens into the hands of a few potentially allows for far better control over liquidity, especially if positive relations can be maintained. It also means the main part of the ICO doesn't need to progress, saving greatly on marketing costs. It is evident ICO approaches will continue to evolve in line with the demands of investors and the opportunities to access funding, meaning advisory services available to support ICO's will become increasingly sophisticated, despite many industry observers declaring the ICO approach all but dead, due to the heavy losses suffered by large numbers of investors in the 2018-19 bear market.

CHAPTER 11
CRYPTO TRADING

ONCE THE ICO is completed and the cryptotoken is launched on an exchange, trading can commence. It is important to note that the vast majority of members who join a cryptotoken loyalty program are unlikely to enter into cryptotoken trading, at least in the early days of this new loyalty approach. They will earn cryptotokens from a participating retailer, watch the value increase and decrease as trading proceeds, then redeem the cryptotokens with a participating retailer for a discount on a transaction. It is likely only the minority will transfer them to an exchange to trade.

That being said, it is both interesting and important for cryptotoken loyalty companies to understand the trading environment in which their cryptotoken is going to be bought and sold and the social media trading communities who obsess about cryptotokens, in order to maximise the opportunities for strong investor support. A consideration for those wishing to gain a crash-course education is to set aside a small amount of money and experiment with trading. This does not constitute trading advice.

The closest parallel to crypto trading is foreign exchange trading. Traders can buy and sell different cryptocurrencies and cryptotokens in the hope they will rise (or fall, if shorting) against other major currencies such as the US dollar and Bitcoin. This is no different to a Forex trader buying UK pounds in the belief their value will rise against the US dollar. The key difference is there are well over one thousand cryptocurrencies and tokens available to trade and the price fluctuations are often extreme, much more so that anything seen on Forex markets.

To start trading, the first step is to set up a digital trading exchange account. There are many to choose from (at the time of writing there are several hundred) and they all have different portfolios of cryptocurrencies and tokens available to trade. Some of the bigger exchanges include Coinbase, Gemini, Poloniex, Bittrex, Kraken, Binance, HitBTC, ShapeShift, Bitfinex, Bitstamp, Cryptopia, OKEx and KuCoin. In choosing an exchange, there are five key factors to consider.

Firstly, location. Where you're located may have a major bearing on what exchanges you can join. Many exchanges have restrictions on residents from certain countries joining, in particular the US. This is because the US has extensive restrictions built into their investment regulations. Only accredited investors can partake in private placements of securities and there is ongoing debate as to whether cryptocurrencies and cryptotokens should be defined as securities or not, although the SEC has indicated they believe most cryptotokens issued via ICO over the past five years to be securities. Fearing future issues from the US government, most exchanges (and ICOs) stay away. Other countries which are often excluded are Singapore and China for similar reasons of enforced government restrictions. North Korea and Iran can also be excluded as cryptocurrencies and tokens can be used to side-step international sanctions, which could cause legal issues for the blockchain company directors.

Secondly, how you want to invest needs to be considered. Some exchanges will only accept deposits of cryptocurrencies, which isn't very useful if you're just starting out and don't own any. Others will accept bank deposits but they can often have limits on them. For example, BTC markets in Australia will only allow deposits of A$2,000 for new accounts. Once a few deposits and trades have been made, they'll increase it to A$8,000 per day. There are also some exchanges which will accept credit card payments, however fees can be high.

Thirdly, what cryptocurrencies to buy is a key consideration. Some exchanges may only offer five to ten different major cryptocurrencies, while others will have hundreds. If the plan is to stick to only trading the majors, such as Bitcoin, Ether, Ripple, LiteCoin, Bitcoin Cash and NEO, then any exchange will do but if a wider portfolio of cryptocurrencies and tokens is desired, it may be necessary to open several exchange accounts.

Fourthly, security is a major consideration. The exchange should have, as a minimum, two factor authentication to protect your account from hackers. Ideally, whenever a trade is made, they should also send an email requesting verification.

Lastly, the trading fees of the exchange should be considered. It is worth comparing fees across different exchanges to get a feel for what is reasonable but, obviously, they should be as low as possible to avoid profits being eaten away. Typically fees vary between exchanges, with many major exchanges charging 0.1-0.5 per cent.

In exploring the trading culture as part of my research for the 1st Edition of *Blockchain Loyalty*, I created accounts with BTC Markets, Cryptopia, KuCoin, OKEx, Binance, HitBTC, Bibox and QRYPTOS in the space of a few weeks in order to chase elusive cryptotokens. One clear opportunity for blockchain companies is to offer their cryptocurrency or cryptotoken for sale on as many exchanges as possible but particularly the major exchanges. This opens up trading volume and can lead to price spikes.

Most exchanges have already implemented a KYC step either as part of the registration process or as a requirement before any funds or crypto can be withdrawn. This ensures compliance with government regulations and requires the member to submit personal details and identification, including photo identification and proof of address. For the bigger exchanges, it can take several days or weeks for the KYC approval and, if especially busy, it may not come at all. Due to excess demand, some exchanges periodically close their doors to new registrations, sometimes permanently. There have even been instances during bull markets where account holders of major exchanges have sold their account to others wanting to get in (in exchange for cryptocurrency, of course).

In addition to setting up an exchange account, it is also prudent to set up a cryptocurrency wallet. Ever since the Mt. Gox exchange closed down in February 2014 after a hack event stole an estimated 850,000 Bitcoin (worth US$450 million at the time), the recommendation from seasoned crypto traders has been to transfer holdings out of the exchanges and keep them in a secure wallet: a software program that stores private and public keys and interacts with various blockchains to enable users to send and receive cryptocurrencies and monitor their balance.

Although traders talk about storing their cryptocurrencies in a wallet, they're actually only storing the record of transaction, as currencies don't get stored in any single location or exist anywhere in physical form. Creating a wallet generates two keys: a private and public key. The public key (or wallet address) is provided to others wishing to send cryptocurrencies or tokens to the wallet. To unlock the wallet the private key must match the public address the currency is assigned to.

There are a range of different crypto wallet options to choose from:

- PC: downloaded onto a PC or laptop and only accessible from that computer. If the computer is lost or destroyed, the wallet will be lost. (By way of interest, James Howell of Wales stored 7,500 Bitcoin on a hard drive which he accidentally threw away, a haul worth over US$82m at February 2018 prices. He later offered the local council 10 per cent of the value if they'd allow him to dig up the landfill in search of the hard drive.[30])

- Online: hosted on the cloud and run by third parties, which makes it more susceptible to hacking and theft but not exposed to hardware issues.

- Mobile: run via an app, and useful for making cryptocurrency transactions.

- Hardware: USB type devices which store everything offline but can be plugged into any computer to access the wallet.

- Paper: includes printing out the public and private keys on a piece of paper to be stored in a secure place. The keys may be printed in the form of QR codes which can then be scanned in the future for transactions, they may be a string of random words which are used to unlock an account.

Once an exchange account is created, a wallet is established and funds have been transferred, the trading can begin. But how does one make sense of this vastly complex landscape and know what to buy?

New investors have a range of options:

---

30 http://www.news.com.au/finance/money/investing/man-who-threw-away-140m-of-bitcoin-wants-to-dig-up-landfill-site/news-story/79b0582630b5dc3ce8cdaf1d373 92ab2

- Join professional investment recommendation companies: Examples include AtomSignal and TurtleBC. They utilise a range of trading prediction methods to identify coins which are likely to increase in value. They also advise clients when to close a trade to lock in any profits or minimise losses.

- Follow traders on social media: A large number of day traders have established cult like followings on social media channels such as Twitter and Reddit. They use charting techniques to predict price rises and falls and provide their recommendations to their fans.

- Charting: As per Forex and stock market trading, charting is being used extensively within the crypto trading world to predict price changes. Many of the exchanges include charting tools and cryptocurrency charting websites, such as Coinigy, which not only provide highly sophisticated charting technology but also the option to link to exchange accounts to make trades and manage stop losses.

- Throw darts at a dartboard.

- Ask the "crypto guy" in the office for some tips.

The other way a trader can buy cryptocurrencies, of course, is via an ICO. The trader has the opportunity to read the company's whitepaper and research their vision, credentials, team, advisors and backers to determine whether they are legitimate and worthy of investment. Investing in an ICO requires registering on the company's website, then transferring the relevant cryptocurrency into a specific account at the right time. The cryptocurrencies which an investor can invest with will often depend on the blockchain platform the cryptotoken is being hosted on. In 2017, most ICOs were run on the Ethereum network, however other platforms such as Waves, Stellar, NEO, NEM, Tron and ICX also support new cryptotokens being launched via ICOs.

Early investors generally receive bonus tokens. During the height of the ICO market, traders were often seen on Twitter sharing links for ICOs, as they received referral fees if their fans click on the link and invest (gamification). Some ICOs were so popular that the companies stopped account registrations early and traders were forced to wait until the token was launched on an exchange before they could buy.

The social media community surrounding cryptocurrency trading is an astounding cultural phenomenon. Extensive conversations abound across Twitter, Facebook, LinkedIn, Telegram, Slack, Bitcointalk, Reddit, Discord and other channels. There are also public and private trading groups which traders can join and meet ups are regularly scheduled around the world where traders can come together and discuss strategies.

In exploring this world, the most compelling social media interaction surely happens on Twitter (or CryptoTwitter (CT) to insiders). A community of day traders have spent the past several years using their charting skills to make predictions on specific cryptocurrencies and have developed extensive followings as a result of their ability to make correct calls. Accounts with pseudonyms such as CryptoHornHairs, KillerWhale, notsofast, CryptoVisionary, Zissou, CryptoDad, The Dog, Altcoin Psycho, TonyTheCryptodealer™, WhalePanda and Blockchain Robot can have followings in excess of 140,000 fans.

They have their own language. Here is a brief glossary:

- Shilling: to promote a coin in the hope the price with rise.

- Mooning: the value of a coin has rapidly risen, i.e. 'to the moon'.

- Shitcoins: tokens which have no utilitarian purpose.

- Noob: new traders who are naïve (derived from new out of the box software) and are derided by the experienced traders.

- HODL: hold their coins irrespective of price volatility. Based on a typo within a social media post by an early Bitcoin trader.[31]

- FUD: Fear Uncertainty Doubt.

They discuss trade profits in terms of lambos (how many Lamborghinis they can buy) and deride the US dollar as the biggest currency rort of all time, particularly with the Federal Reserve Bank printing money as part of quantitative easing. They laugh at CNBC showing viewers how to buy Ripple at its peak and sell at the bottom and deride Warren Buffet for saying cryptocurrencies won't last. They talk extensively of Whales (traders who bought into cryptocurrencies early in the game and made fortunes in the hundreds of millions or billions). Part of an early network committed to ensuring cryptocurrencies succeeded, some of them have allegedly formed syndicates which coordinate large buys and sells on particular coins to influence the price and

---

31 https://bitcointalk.org/index.php?topic=375643.0?red

profit handsomely. It is rumoured the Whales stimulate FUD to drive a coin's price down, then buy up big and drive the price up, causing FOMO buying panic amongst noobs, which then moons the coin.

One important role the day traders play is to provide community advice on reducing trading risk. The cultural interactions are in many ways similar to neotribal formations by drug users frequenting dance events. Dr Katherine Ireland studied the sociality of dance events and how belonging to a social network was often used as a basis for risk reduction.[32] She found in particular that self-care was 'a social practice, enmeshed in social relationships and networks of communication. Analysis of partygoers' accounts indicated how, in these stories, forms of small friendship networks, large crowd and ecstatic belongings were produced and how drug use was regulated through techniques of self-care and guiding discourses.'

Dr Ireland also determined that 'drug use was regulated through techniques of self-care, in the form of preparation, sharing in pleasure of drugs, support and information, guided by the key principle of "balance" in relation to the condition of the embodied self, atmospheric space, rhythm and activities of events and everyday life and relationships.' This is very much the landscape of trader interactions on Twitter (and other social media channels) which presents a fascinating case study of digital neotribalism.

In an environment where many traders are new, the rules are unclear and the amount of guidance material is limited, the crypto Twitter community plays a central and crucial role in advising novices (noobs) and reminding experts on techniques for minimising the inherent risks involved in trading in a highly volatile market. Experienced traders educate on basic charting skills, the importance of placing stop losses and the most critical reminder of all, 'don't panic,' when the market takes a sudden dip. They recommend other traders to follow via Follow Fridays (or #FF), advise against ICOs which appear to be scams and engage in healthy debates about the merits of investing in one coin or token over another. Some of them create educational documents, videos and podcasts to share their knowledge further proving they are fundamental aspects of the ecosystem.

'Actually putting in the work to study market cycles, coin fundamentals, basic TA, etc will put you above 95 per cent of the other people involved in

---

32 Ireland, K., 'The sociality of dance events and health implications,' UNSW, 2002

crypto,' tweeted Crypto Boss. 'Most people are lazy and are relying on others to spoon feed them what coins to buy and when. Don't be one of those people.'

'Go too fast, ya bound to crash,' CryptoHornHairs tweeted. 'Scaling in buys & sells was 1 of the most valuable breakthroughs I had in my trading career. To elaborate; when buying dips, don't go all in @ a certain price, distribute buy orders down the scale price, making your buys fatter as price drops.'

The social media communities also provide lots of moral support when market conditions don't go according to plan.

As the market started plummeting in early 2018, The Digital Currency Advisor tweeted, 'I don't own a bunch of shit coins so I'm not going to sell anything during a correction. I'm also not going to take a loss to chase something else that's moving. I've been through several of these. #crypto markets bounce back quickly after sell offs. Be patient and #HOLD.' Six hours later after the market had hit the bottom and started to quickly recover he followed up with, 'I used the dip to buy cryptos on sale, I will add quality coins during each dip. Day trading during a correction, or selling to chase a coin that's moving is how you get rekt. Now's the time if you have additional capital to go shopping. When this thing bounces it will be fast.' After hitting bottom, the market was up 40 per cent within 12 hours, demonstrating the extreme volatility of cryptocurrency trading.

HODL as a trading strategy turned out to be extremely flawed, demonstrating the limitations of using this type of investor community to make trading decisions. With most cryptocurrencies and cryptotokens down over 98% from peaks, those investors who chose to HODL have suffered enormous losses which (at least in the short-term) they are unlikely to recover.

An essential role within a blockchain loyalty program is that of the Investor Communications team. While points and miles coalition loyalty program operators need to manage relationships with their members and retailers, blockchain loyalty program operators have the additional complication of managing their cryptotoken investor base.

Most blockchain companies use a variety of social media channels to make regular announcements to their community of investors to keep them feeling positive about the potential of the company and reduce the likelihood they'll sell their cryptocurrency or cryptotoken allocation. This includes roadmap strategies, platform development updates, new exchange listings, company partnerships, conference presentations and more. Staff working in this area who have gained exposure to trading and the crypto-trading community have an advantage in that they understand the types of messages which will resonate, the channels which are most powerful and the appropriate language to use. This team is also responsible for attracting new investors to the cryptotoken, which involves running digital marketing and social media promotions, recruiting key influencers and generating effective PR campaigns.

CHAPTER 12
CRYPTOTOKEN LOYALTY ANALYTICS AND MEMBER LIFECYCLE MANAGEMENT

WITH THE CRYPTOTOKEN loyalty program successfully launched and a growing member base earning cryptotokens via retailer transactions and other activities, it is important to implement a member lifecycle management process. This will serve to facilitate an effective communications and rewards strategy to maintain engagement and grow interactions with the program.

A member lifecycle management strategy involves using analytics to develop a segmentation model, where different segments can be managed in a way which recognises their current lifecycle position while attempting to transition them to a more ideal lifecycle segment.

AN EFFECTIVE MEMBER lifecycle management strategy can enable powerful customer interaction approaches that generate significant business growth, profitability and competitive differentiation.

Most companies have a lifecycle marketing strategy which looks like this:

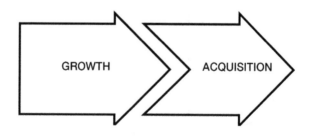

The focus is limited to two areas: convincing members to join the program, then bombarding them with promotional emails to drive sales.

I studied one program for a mid-sized retailer. They mandated their retail staff to sign up as many customers as possible to their loyalty program and were very successful with this approach. On average 70 per cent of their transactions were made by members of their loyalty program, with some stores experiencing 100 per cent of their transactions by members. Once a member joined the program, they received an email almost every day and everyone received the same email. It was marketing assault at an extreme level. The engagement data showed the approach wasn't working. Dismally, email open rates were below ten per cent and unsubscribe rates were over two per cent for each email. Sales resulting from an email were rarely more than A$5,000 to A$10,000. Despite success in signing up customers to the program, each week they were seeing their marketing database shrink as more members opted out of communications than joined the program.

From the members' perspective, the rapid disengagement wasn't very surprising. It was an unpleasant experience of signing up to a loyalty program only to be bombarded with emails promoting stuff they didn't want. Fortunately, the company took my advice and restructured their approach to turn the situation around. The key was the development of a member lifecycle management strategy which helped them adopt a more tailored and personalised communications approach for their member base, meaning they no longer felt the need to email all members with the same offer every day.

A more evolved member lifecycle management approach looks like this:

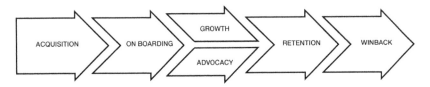

Acquisition

As discussed in Chapter 4, simplicity is key to loyalty program engagement. The program should be simple to join, understand and engage with. Opening an account with a trading exchange and creating a digital wallet and transferring money to the exchange to buy one of many cryptocurrency trading pairs isn't simple, which is what provides blockchain loyalty with so much potential for mainstreaming cryptotoken ownership. If a member can join a program with their name, an email address and a password and start earning cryptotokens immediately, then a powerful dynamic has been created: one which will be familiar to them, fast to process and carry no risk (as they're not investing any of their own money). The key design flaw of most loyalty programs is only providing a single option for members to join the program, such as picking up a plastic card in store then heading online to fill in a registration form. Superior programs provide multiple ways for a member to join. Here's a best practice design which allows members to join via a variety of ways, allowing them to choose the one which best suits their needs:

Physical membership card

The member can grab a membership card in store and provide their email address to the cashier. They can scan their new card to earn tokens for their transaction. They receive an email with a link which directs them to the online registration page to complete their registration. Alternatively the cashier can capture all their details and complete the registration on the spot.

Digital member card

The member texts their first name to a short code and receives a link in reply. They're directed to the registration page to complete the process, with their first name already populated. They can also download a digital card to their favourite digital wallet app, such as Apple Wallet or GPay. Alternatively, they can use their mobile number to identify for future transactions.

Online

The member can create an account online either directly on the website or when transacting online with a retail partner. The member will be sent a link to download a digital member card to their mobile, which they can scan when making in store transactions. They will also be invited to download the program app.

Biometric scan

The member scans a fingerprint, face or eye or records a voiceprint. They provide their email address or mobile number to the cashier. They're sent a link to the registration page to complete the process. They also earn on that transaction.

App

The member downloads the loyalty program's app and registers. The app may contain a barcode, NFC or other swipe-based transaction features. They may also be able to store credit or debit cards on the app, which allows them to identify as a member when paying without having to swipe a separate card.

Credit or debit cards

The member can join the program and link their account to their credit or debit card. When paying with the card at participating retailers, the transaction is automatically captured, meaning there's no need for another member card or app download.

Stored value card or personal ID

Travel cards (such as Oyster in the UK and MetroCard in New York) also have the potential to be used as a replacement membership card. Some countries such as Sweden even provide the opportunity for driver's licences to be used via retailer access to a public database. The member scans the card and provides their email address, and receives an email with a link to the registration page to complete the join process.

Blockchain ID

Estonia has moved their entire citizen identification database onto a blockchain platform[33], which has the potential to provide another option for loyalty program member transactions.

---

33 https://medium.com/e-residency-blog/
welcome-to-the-blockchain-nation-5d9b46c06fd4

Blockchain is advanced technology, so the expectation of members will be that technological innovation will extend to all aspects of the program design. With the join process being the first interaction the member has with the program, it is important to take advantage of the opportunity to show them they have been placed at the centre of the design process.

On-boarding

Lincoln Murphy, author of *Customer Success: How Innovative Companies Are Reducing Churn and Growing Recurring Revenue*, once said, 'The seeds of churn are planted early.' This is particularly true of a loyalty program, where early meaningful interactions can have a profound impact on the engagement longevity of a member. It is especially true for a blockchain loyalty program, where the complexity of the cryptotoken has the potential to generate member confusion if they aren't adequately educated early in their lifecycle, particularly around the propensity for the currency to fluctuate. For any company, it is important to determine what an early win looks like for a customer. For example, if a customer successfully registers, earns tokens, then redeems those tokens for a reward, they could be seen to have achieved a win. They've been around the earn and redeem cycle once and now they likely understand how the program works and ideally will be thinking about how to access their next win. How then can the loyalty program operator help the new member to secure that win as early in their lifecycle as possible? The key is effective educational communication, which is delivered via a well-designed on-boarding process. Here are some suggested options:

- New loyalty program members who demonstrate early engagement with the program are much more likely to remain engaged. This is particularly true if the engagement is reinforced with an early reward. One option is to reward them with some bonus tokens for completing the registration and making their first transaction.

- The on-boarding process is critical to ensure the new member feels adequately educated about the program and suitably rewarded for their early engagement. Running focus groups with members to seek feedback on communication styles is advised to ensure the message is clear and understandable.

- Utilising A/B testing, different rewards and offers, in-store recognition and different communication channels will help improve the quality of the on-boarding process, leading to deeper member engagement earlier in the lifecycle and reducing the propensity for future churn.

- A refined on-boarding communications process requires measuring how members interact with the communications and adjusting accordingly using trigger and behavioural based email rules.

- An advanced on-boarding process identifies what type of segment the customer is and aligns them to a tailored messaging framework. Different segments will respond to different stimuli, therefore adjusting communications based on who the customer is and what they engage with will increase the chances of successful education.

Growth

The primary ambition of a loyalty program is to generate deeper engagement from the member with the brand, leading to a greater share of wallet spend. The opportunities to stimulate growth via a well designed loyalty program are endless. Specific to cryptotoken loyalty, the biggest carrot to grow member transactions is their desire to earn more cryptotokens, so a variety of campaigns should be designed around this. It is equally important to ensure the communications approach is adequately personalised so that members only receive offers which are immediately relevant to them. The more advanced loyalty programs utilise highly specialised personalisation engines to automatically generate member communications. Each week, they load hundreds of offers into the engine and based on a variety of factors (demographic, previous transactions, survey responses, time of day and more) individualised sets of emails are created for each member.

Alongside cryptotoken loyalty, some of the main trends evolving to drive growth include:

Convergence

Western companies are desperately trying to replicate the success of Chinese apps such as WeChat, which have managed to converge a vast range of services into a single app, such as banking, bookings, transport, messaging, rewards and more. The opportunity for blockchain loyalty is an app which can be used within the program to earn the loyalty cryptotoken, store credit cards and other loyalty cards, store and buy/sell other major cryptocurrencies and tokens, redeem at POS and more.

Convenience

Companies have an incredible opportunity to save members time by streamlining the transaction experience and facilitating rapid delivery. No company does this better than Amazon but other companies doing this well include BWS in Australia (one hour chilled alcohol deliveries) and Hilton (with a booking app which becomes the room key, thereby bypassing the check in desk). In a world where time is valued almost as much as money, those companies that save people time will create a significant strategic advantage. Cryptotoken loyalty has the opportunity to deliver a streamlined checkout experience at retail partners by making the payment process rapid and seamless, in the same way Walmart has used their payment app to fast track their customer's purchases.

Experience

Retailers are transforming their stores into destinations which members are drawn to, taking them beyond the transactional process. Nordstrom has a clothing store with no clothes, where customers can enjoy champagne while they shop and have their purchases shipped directly to their house. REI has a rock climbing pinnacle, where customers can try out their equipment and enjoy the best views of Seattle. Laphroaig members can journey to their distillery on the Isle of Islay to visit their personal one square foot plot of land and claim their rent (one free dram of the world's finest whisky). With a coalition cryptotoken loyalty program, the program operator has the opportunity to work with the retail partners to create an exclusive in store experience just for program members in order to build an emotional connection with the brand.

"Me-commerce"

Major brands are working harder and harder to place the member at the centre of the retail universe, including using identification devices such as in-store Wi-Fi to segment customers and tailor the service offering. The individualised communication approaches are primarily being driven by personalisation engines (which will eventually be AI controlled) but another future paradigm is blockchain marketing which is covered in the next chapter.

Social

There are very few loyalty program operators around the world who are utilising social well, despite its massive potential as a communication channel to drive customer growth and connection. The opportunity for cryptotoken loyalty is the passion people feel towards cryptocurrencies and tokens, as evidenced with Crypto Twitter and other channels. A cryptotoken loyalty program has the potential to develop a significant following by members and investors alike. The momentum is naturally created with the ICO and can be expanded from there in a way that points and miles based programs would never be able to replicate. This involves cleverly utilising all available channels, including harnessing rapidly expanding messaging applications such as Facebook Messenger.

Advocacy

The most efficient and cost effective method for a loyalty program to attract new members and grow engagement is via member advocacy. It is surprising that loyalty program operators don't focus more resources on building advocacy. The easiest way to accomplish this is by incentivising members to write positive reviews about the program, as well as incentivising them to follow and share on social media. For a cryptotoken loyalty company the opportunity is greater because the desire for the currency and the passion for the program has the potential to be more intense, which makes it much easier to harness the power of the member base in promoting the program to their family, friends and followers. The blockchain gamification methods detailed in Chapter 9 can be applied with great effect to inspire the member base to become advocates, helping to build the community effect which is so important for the rapid expansion of a coalition loyalty program. It's very common to see crypto investors promoting the coins and tokens they've invested in to try and encourage more people to buy in. This is often a form of community service ('this coin is going to moon, so buy it now and you'll get rich') and personal ambition ('if more people buy this coin the value of my holding will increase'). A number of blockchain companies are utilising concepts such as Airdrops (where they reward people for engaging with them via social media or holding their currency) and paid referrals (where influencers are provided with a sum of cryptotokens to shill or promote their company and currency to their followers) as a way to capitalise on advocacy networks.

Retention

An important role of the marketing team within a loyalty program is to monitor member engagement and identify members who are showing signs of disengagement. These signs can often be a precursor to the member ceasing any involvement with the program altogether, so it is important for the program to respond as early as possible with quality retention activity. Good quality analytics will allow the program to determine clear warning signs. One such sign is where the member spends their entire balance on a reward and doesn't quickly follow up with more earn activity. To offset the loss of a valuable member, the loyalty program team needs to do their best to understand why the member is behaving in that way and do their best to reengage them with whatever it takes: rectifying an issue, providing better service, matching a competitor's offer or providing a value injection. With the rise of blockchain loyalty programs additional issues are likely to arise which will require retention responses; they may not understand why their account balance keeps changing due to value fluctuations or there may be a dip in the market which significantly reduces their balance. It's important for the program operator to take the time to tease out all the potential irritants which may trigger a disengagement event, implement analytics to track and identify affected members, have solid strategies in place to address the challenges, and even turn them into positives.

Winback

Members can choose to completely cease interaction with a program for a variety of reasons. The primary reason is they don't perceive they are accessing meaningful value and may not feel an emotional connection with the brand. They may find interacting with the program to be too complicated and onerous. Sometimes there is nothing the program can do to rectify their disengagement from some customers. For example, frequent flyer programs often see complete disengagement from once frequent travellers who have changed their career path (different role or retirement) or life path and no longer need to fly regularly, if at all. The airline can throw lots of money at the customer to try to offset the identified disengagement but it's wasted resources, so knowing *why* the customer is disengaging will help the airline save their retention budget. Inevitably, a program will end up with a percentage of their member base who are completely inactive but the opportunity still exists for the program to attempt to win them back. Even a highly successful coalition loyalty program can have 30 to 40 per cent of its member base inactive. This process needs to start with experimentation. If the analytics are unable to provide guidance on why the member left, there's not much the program can do to address the issues other than via segmentation approaches. A progressive blockchain loyalty company would begin by creating a list of all the possible value they can provide to these lapsed members in return for reengagement. It may be a double token bonus if they complete a transaction with a retailer, bonus tokens for filling in a survey or even a bonus for updating their account details. They key is to stimulate simple engagement from the member, then build on the successful response.

The presented member lifecycle management model is relatively simple. More complex models are also possible, where the segments are more granular, allowing for even better insight and communication approaches. This type of model has standard acquisition and on-boarding segments but members are segmented into whether they have made a single purchase or multiple purchases. Multiple purchase members can be further divided in to growth, stable or decline segments or even in to status tiers based on spend within a specified time period. These types of models are very transaction based and don't consider any psychographic insight, meaning they can indicate what the member is doing but cannot answer why.

The holy grail is an AI powered personalisation engine which generates one to one communications with the member based on a variety of transactional, demographic and psychographic information. A quality cryptotoken loyalty company should certainly have a roadmap to move the program towards this type of model.

CHAPTER 13

CRYPTOTOKEN LOYALTY PROGRAM TECHNOLOGY

As THE CORE differentiating feature of a cryptotoken loyalty program is the use of a cryptotoken instead of points and miles, the technology stack required can encompass a hybrid solution of on-chain and off-chain technology, with most of the day-to-day processing conducted by a good-quality non-block-chain loyalty platform. The basic approach involves connecting a standard loyalty platform to a blockchain platform which can support cryptotokens (such as Ethereum, NEO, NEM and EOS), plus support a secure blockchain data wallet for the blockchain marketing element.

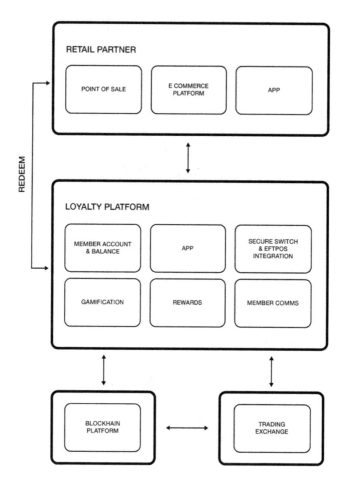

Loyalty platforms used to be expensive and inflexible, but these days there are a number of high-quality white label platforms available around the world. My experience has been that the older the platform, the more expensive and inflexible it's likely to be. Some of the best platforms I've seen are less than five years old, have been designed for easy API integration with other systems and provide highly complex campaign capability, app and digital wallet support, automated personalisation engine marketing capabilities and extensive analytics smarts.

I once ran a tender process for a client to help them find a loyalty platform vendor. During a presentation session, I asked one of the vendors if their system could perform a certain task. One of their developers jumped on his laptop, wrote some quick code, loaded it and with a smile replied, 'It can now.' Suffice to say, they won the tender!

A good quality loyalty platform should be able to deliver across four core areas.

Loyalty

Not surprisingly, the platform should be able to do all the basics, which includes supporting the creation of a member account, adding loyalty currency to the account and allowing the member to redeem the cryptotoken. It should also be able to support status tiers and provide status benefits to those members such as bonus currency and access to exclusive products or services. It should also be able to take feeds from third party platforms via API or batch data if the program supports earn from other companies.

Almost all loyalty platforms can support these features.

Engagement

This is where the quality platforms are separated from the ordinary platforms. A loyalty platform is ultimately a rules engine and the good ones can support incredibly complex rules. The loyalty program operator should be able to pump in lots of different transaction data (such as the date and time, product SKU, cost, retailer) and personal data (such as a member identifier, demographic data and status tier) and have the platform apply a range of rules in real time to deliver a variety of specified outcomes. This may be bonus currency, cashback, new status tiers, free tickets or many other outcomes.

The best platforms can support multi step campaigns, whereby the member must complete a series of transactions and tasks to unlock a benefit, with each step being tracked and recorded as they go. This type of platform allows for advanced gamification and is useful for supporting automated member lifecycle marketing approaches. The best will have a machine-learning personalisation engine incorporated to generate complex one to one marketing communications.

Rewards

For a traditional loyalty program rewards are generally localised, with gift cards and consumer products sourced from local suppliers and shipped to local members. Major coalition loyalty programs with a global presence often struggle to deliver a consistent reward offering at an international level. The biggest access to the reward range will be in their home country, with a limited supply available to overseas members. The best example of this is frequent flyer programs, which may offer flights and an online store in their home country but only flights in other countries, due to the logistics involved in sourcing and shipping internationally.

Ideally the platform provider will be able to access a quality range of rewards for the country in which the program is operating, however the loyalty industry has evolved extensively over the last decade and many businesses now play the role of reward consolidators, offering large ranges and handling all the dropship logistics for fulfilment. This has made accessing sizeable rewards ranges quite easy. Thus, rewards range shouldn't be a major factor in determining the viability of the platform.

From a cryptotoken loyalty perspective the reward is the cryptotoken, so other rewards are less relevant, making this program design very well suited to international expansion.

Payments

Increasingly, loyalty platform providers are stepping into the payments space as they chase convergence of technology and aim to own the transaction. This streamlines processing and allows for real time earn and redemption.

Most of the big coalition programs still run on batch processing; the retailer sends them a data file of the member transactions once a month, the program operator loads it into their platform, the points or miles are deposited into the member's account and the operator sends the retailer an invoice to cover the cost of the points. This means long delays for the member to receive their points, plus additional administration for the program operator to process reject files, raise invoices and chase for payment.

The smarter platform providers are taking control of the payment by either controlling the EFTPOS terminal (allowing them to deduct the cost of the points from the payment then hand the rest over to the retailer) or creating smart apps with virtual credit card features (where the member pays via the app and the platform deducts the cost of the points as a credit card transaction fee). These are incredibly significant features for blockchain loyalty because the expectation of members will be earning their cryptotokens instantly. With a highly fluctuating currency, members don't want to wait four to six weeks to receive their tokens in case the price 'moons' in the interim period.

This set up also facilitates a more streamlined redemption process as well. With an app connected to a virtual credit card, the member can instantly sell their cryptotoken holding within the app and make a payment to the retailer in real time. Imagine walking into a store, selecting your products, opening the app at the checkout, cashing in enough cryptotokens to cover the cost of the purchase and walking out. In the background, the platform has conducted a real time transaction with an exchange to sell the allocation of cryptotokens and credit the fiat directly to the retailer. The cryptotokens used may be the ones linked to the loyalty program (which the member has accumulated from previous transactions) or it may be other cryptocurrencies they've accumulated elsewhere, such as Bitcoin, Ether and NEO. Streamlining this payment processing approach solves an existing shortcoming of cryptocurrencies and cryptotokens, which is the ability to easily access them and use them as part of everyday spend. By addressing this within the context of a loyalty program the program operator delivers the potential for a net inflow of cryptocurrency into the program, a considerable benefit for retail partners.

Once a platform has been secured, the next step is to connect it to a blockchain platform. While there are many blockchain platforms to consider, the most important considerations are the ability to create a new token, fast processing times and low (or no) transaction fees. One blockchain which definitely doesn't fit this criterion is the Bitcoin platform, which can be slow and expensive to transact and doesn't support new cryptotokens. Ethereum supports many cryptotokens and has supported the largest number of ICOs but it can also be slow to process transactions and, depending on the load, the transaction fees can be high. NEO and NEM are supporting new ICOs with solid and reputable platforms and many new players have entered this space including ICX, CoinList, Republic, TokenSoft, Indiegogo, ICO Engine, BlockEx, EOS, Komodo, Stellar and Cointopia.

Additionally, the platform must be connected to a reputable and reliable trading exchange to buy and sell cryptotokens as required.

The ideal transaction flow works as follows.

The platform connects directly to the retail partners systems via API to collect transaction data. If the POS is old and cannot support an API connection, the retailer may choose to use something like a PiCo-POS terminal; a simple plug and play requiring no changes to the core system.

When transacting with a retailer, the member scans their unique barcode or pays via the credit card stored in the app to identify. The loyalty platform collects the member number, product SKU data and amount paid per product (basket level data) and applies the rules engine to determine the value of cryptotokens the member is entitled to. A transaction is processed via the blockchain platform and the digital trading exchange to purchase the tokens on the member's behalf at the live market rate. The tokens are deposited into the member's account, where the member can view them via the app, website or digital membership card on their mobile.

Members may also be able to earn cryptotokens by transacting with an extensive network of affiliate partners. By signing into their online account, or accessing the app, members can browse the network of partners and click through to their website to transact. On completing a transaction, the affiliate partner pays the loyalty program operator a percentage of the total spent as affiliate marketing revenue. The loyalty program operator uses this revenue to purchase cryptotokens from the digital trading exchange on the member's behalf.

Under a blockchain marketing structure, members may also be able to earn cryptotokens for agreeing to receive promotions from their favourite brands, determined by analysing the basket level transaction data collected from retail partners. The loyalty program operator will negotiate with relevant brands to send a promotional communication via the loyalty platform to members, who will receive a small amount of cryptotokens if they view and engage with the promotional offer and bonus cryptotokens if they take it up. The cost of the cryptotokens will be paid for by the brand. The loyalty program can use the promotional revenue to purchase cryptotokens from the digital trading exchange on the member's behalf.

The loyalty platform should allow for a wide range of sophisticated gamification approaches to encourage the member to build out their personal profile by providing bonus cryptotoken offers to reward members for providing personal details, linking social media accounts, following the loyalty program on social media, filling in surveys, playing games, inviting family and friends to join and much more. The loyalty program operator may also decide to include status tiers for higher value members, a standard feature of most loyalty platforms.

Members can redeem cryptotokens in store at retail partners using the app or a linked credit card. The app allows the member to view their cryptotoken balance and the live market value based on the actual exchange rate. They can choose the amount they wish to spend and the correct amount will automatically be sold on the exchange, with the equivalent cash amount (less transaction fees) deposited into their digital wallet or directly to the retailer. Utilising the speed of the blockchain platform will allow this transaction to be processed in a fraction of a second for a fraction of a cent, ensuring the payment process isn't delayed and the member isn't left frustrated. It also ensures the retailer never needs to hold the cryptotokens, which insulates them from any value fluctuation risks.

Members can sign in to the retail partner's online account and shop as normal. At the checkout stage, the website will display their cryptotoken balance. The member will be able to pay using fiat currency, cryptotokens or a combination. The amount of cryptotokens chosen will be automatically sold on the exchange, with the equivalent cash amount paid directly to the retail partner.

Members can transfer their cryptotokens to their own personal digital wallet and use them to buy cryptocurrencies and tokens or sell for cash on participating exchanges. When processing the transfer, the member enters their personal digital wallet address and the transaction is added to the secure ledger on the blockchain platform, with the member's loyalty program account showing a subsequent deduction.

Call centre agents have access to member account details to provide full support as required across phone, email, chat or app for both members and retailers. One of the main decisions a blockchain loyalty company needs to make when implementing the technical solution is whether to provide the member with a blockchain wallet or a standard loyalty account. Existing blockchain loyalty companies are differing on which solution to implement, therefore it is important both are explored. The simplest option is to provide the member with a standard loyalty account. Under this approach, when the member earns cryptotokens, the system purchases from the exchange and holds the cryptotokens in a central wallet and informs the member they have an allocation. The member can access their account and see they have cryptotokens available, but they are not physically stored in their account. This approach is the same as a prepaid debit card. While the user of the card perceives they have fiat currency stored in an individual account linked to the card, the fiat is actually stored in a single bank account along with the holdings of all other users. The advantage of this approach is it doesn't require the creation of millions of crypto wallets, saving on cost.

The more advanced option is to provide each member with their own wallet. The wallet can be hosted on an exchange or on a blockchain platform, and each time the member earns cryptotokens they are deposited into the wallet. While more complicated and costly to implement, the provision of a member controlled cryptowallet easily allows them to store, and transact with, other cryptocurrencies. Thus, the loyalty program can extend into a program which allows for a variety of crypto transactions. One company that has implemented this approach is EZToken, who have their own exchange which they host member wallets on. Their vision is a program which allows members to earn and redeem EZToken with retailers, but also buy and sell other cryptocurrencies such as Bitcoin and Ether, as well as transferring cryptocurrencies to other members and trading on the EZToken Exchange. Such approaches are set to play a key role in mainstreaming cryptocurrency adoption, all done within the familiar framework of a loyalty program model which has existed for centuries.

CHAPTER 14

ENTERPRISE BLOCKCHAIN LOYALTY SOLUTIONS

THUS FAR, *BLOCKCHAIN Loyalty* has focused on four main areas, all of which involve the use of cryptocurrencies and cryptotokens:

1. A loyalty program powered by a single new cryptotoken

2. A loyalty program powered by an existing cryptocurrency

3. Many loyalty programs powered by multiple new cryptotokens on a single platform

4. A security token supported by a loyalty program

This chapter will focus on the fifth area, which has the potential to deliver more benefits to the loyalty industry than the other four combined, all without the use of cryptocurrencies.

5. A loyalty program enhanced by an enterprise blockchain solution

As discussed in the Introduction, a blockchain platform can be integrated with a loyalty platform, as well as earn and redemption partner platforms, to facilitate secure, real-time and auto-reconciled transactions, an approach which provides particular advantages for major loyalty programs that have large, expensive legacy systems. Legacy loyalty platforms often lack flexibility, limiting the ability of the loyalty program operators to innovate with new campaign concepts. A back-end blockchain platform connected to the legacy system can allow campaign rules to be exported, allowing the operator to more easily execute complex campaigns without having to develop or replace their expensive system. This can also allow for easier on-boarding of earn and redemption partners and more efficient processing of transactions, thereby reducing administrative overheads.

The global leader in this area is Loyyal (*www.loyyal.com*). Founded in 2014, *Loyyal* is an enterprise-grade Blockchain as a Service (BaaS) platform with a significant client portfolio including a major middle-eastern airline, *Star Alliance*, *Deloitte*, a large Canadian bank, *Hawk Incentives* (a *Blackhawk Network* company) and *Bond Brand Loyalty*. Loyalty & Reward Co were engaged as consultants in late 2018 by Australian company Reffind, a 15% stakeholder of Loyyal, which provided us with the opportunity to gain access to the team and platform to really understand the company's potential.

Loyyal's patented *Hyperledger*-based platform is designed to extend and enhance existing CRM, loyalty and enterprise resource planning (ERP) platforms rather than replace them, an astute strategy considering the millions of dollars many programs have invested in their legacy systems. Importantly, Loyyal avoid competing with these program operators by not playing in the cryptotoken loyalty space. This is a smart move, particularly in light of the struggles facing cryptotoken loyalty programs that are failing to grow their merchant and member bases while suffering large-scale crashes in their cryptotoken prices.

Loyyal's grand vision is to build the Internet of Loyalty®; a global permissioned blockchain of program operators connected to a large base of earn and redemption partners. Any business connecting to the Loyyal platform will be able to automatically access any other business that is connected (providing that permission has been granted).

Loyalty program operators face a range of challenges. Current loyalty legacy technology is expensive to manage, scale and integrate. Any significant innovation is generally constrained by fragmented technology. The onboarding of earn and redemption partners can be complex, slow and expensive, especially if supporting real-time earn. Program interoperability, such as the processing of earn and redemption transactions between airline partners, involves inefficient, varied protocols which require entire teams to manage them.

Furthermore, coalition loyalty transactional processes are based on 1980's designs, back when frequent flyer programs were first invented. Loyalty program operators struggle with reject and reconciliation issues caused by data mismatches, which require significant manual processing, costing time and revenue. On the member experience side, points and miles can take up to 30 days to hit accounts in an era where immediacy is a consumer expectation.

There are an estimated US$500bn of points and miles in circulation and over 3.8bn loyalty accounts in the US alone. In this massive, global loyalty industry, small efficiency gains can deliver multi-million dollar benefits, making Loyyal's platform potentially very valuable to major loyalty program operators.

The Loyyal platform integrates with existing legacy loyalty systems to deliver faster onboarding of new earn and redemption partners, streamlined reconciliation and settlement processes and simplified data sharing among partners with reduced IT time and effort. It also supports the enablement of multi-program promotions more easily with shared liability, the ability to develop broader insight into member behaviours (including across partner programs) and the capacity to generate real-time, targeted promotions.

One company utilising Loyyal is a major middle-eastern airline that has managed to replace their two-way cumbersome reconciliation and verification process with a single step, a solution which saves them and their partners countless hours and revenue, while improving the member experience by reducing the incidence of errors.

Another company connected to the Loyyal platform is Hawk Incentives, a subsidiary of Blackhawk network, the largest supplier of gift cards in the world. Rather than having to connect to individual loyalty platforms, any loyalty operator connecting to the Loyyal platform can now allow their points and miles to be redeemed on Hawk Incentive gift cards. Programs can choose to offer physical or electronic gift cards from over 120 brands or Visa/MasterCard prepaid debit cards.

Loyyal are operating on a global level with a presence in the US, UK, Europe, Middle East, Asia and Australia/NZ. Their reach includes reseller partnerships with *IBM, Deloitte, Cap Gemini* and REFFIND.

I interviewed Gregory Simon, CEO and Founder of Loyyal Corporation regarding his inspiration for starting Loyyal and his thoughts on blockchain loyalty.

'The inspiration was my personal experience in being confused and frustrated with existing loyalty programs. The ability for blockchain to potentially move value efficiently and securely was an obvious solution to some of the underlying causes. Most of the industry will remain as actively-managed branded programs. These programs are the bulk of the industry for a simple reason; consumers are loyal to the brands they interact with and consume. I believe operators of branded programs will adopt blockchain technology as their underlying architecture. This does not make loyalty points cryptocurrencies, however. Eventually, the entire industry will be blockchain-based and nobody will notice. If done properly, the consumer need not even know blockchain is powering their favourite loyalty programs. It will disappear in the background, just as the internet has behind our smartphones and TVs. Points are still points, only better.'

Loyyal are also successfully securing patents around the world. In December 2018, they announced a new patent had been approved in Japan. The award by the Japanese Patent Office of Patent for *Distributed Ledger Protocol to Incentivize Transactional and Non-Transactional Commerce* was yet another addition to Loyyal's growing portfolio of intellectual property, alongside other associated patents at various stages of approval in over eight territories globally.

'Having the scope of this innovation recognized by the Japanese Patent Office is a major step forward for Loyyal,' said Thom Kozik, Loyyal's Chief Commercial Officer. 'Given the innovation and leadership Japanese firms have historically shown in consumer loyalty programs in the retail sector and elsewhere, we are excited about the new opportunities and partnerships this opens for Loyyal in Japan, and in Asia at large.'

Soon after receiving the patent approval, Loyyal secured investment from Japanese firm Recruit Co., Ltd. Recruit is a $40bn market cap Japanese company with a dominant presence in the HR, Media and Solution, and Staffing Services technologies. Recruit has strong brand name recognition in Japan. Using Loyyal, Recruit plans to aggressively enter the Japan incentive management industry, which kicked off in March 2019 at Recruit's annual conference in Tokyo.

Japan is the second largest loyalty market in the world and very invested in the future potential of blockchain. Loyyal is well-placed to capture a sizeable share of the market with their world-class enterprise blockchain loyalty platform.

As mentioned earlier, Loyyal's tech stack is designed to enhance, rather than replace, legacy loyalty platforms:

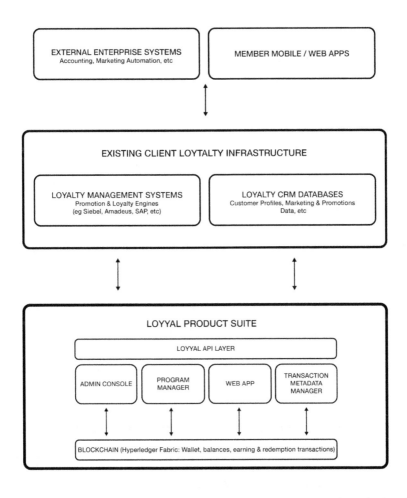

An API layer connects to the legacy loyalty platform, providing the loyalty program operator with access to an Admin Console (providing basic member management capabilities and operational metrics such as overall transaction volume and processing velocity) and Program Manager. The Program Manager enables the definition and configuration of incentives and other aspects of an incentive campaign. It also allows for management of member balances and other data, providing the security controls to selectively share that information with earn and redemption partners.

Interestingly, Loyyal are not the only company operating in this space.

AMEX has implemented a blockchain solution which allows retailers to create smart contracts to fulfil reward program offers. When offers are made to cardholders, the smart contract sends information about the transaction to AMEX and the private blockchain network anonymously so that it can't be traced back to individual cardholders.

Accenture and KPMG have developed blockchain solutions to make it easier for frequent flyer program members to redeem their miles. Accenture developed a solution for AsiaMiles, while KPMG developed a solution for Singapore Airlines.

With KPMG, Singapore Airlines Krisflyer loyalty program launched KrisPay in mid-2018. The digital wallet app is accessible for KrisFlyer members and uses blockchain technology to enable travellers to spend their miles at retail establishments, hotels, petrol stations and other retail partners. Singapore Airlines CEO Goh Choon Phong stated, 'By creating a miles-based digital wallet which integrates the use of miles into their daily lives, KrisFlyer members have yet another way to use miles instantly on everyday transactions.' The wallet allows members to transact using as little as 15 KrisPay miles to pay for their purchases at partner merchants. Although the KPMG solution tokenises the miles, they use a static value token tied to the value of Krisflyer miles.

UK-based *Supermoney* are recent entrants to this space, but come with a grand vision after completing accelerator programs with *BMW Financial Services* and Volvo where they developed a unique digital wallet allowing in-store and online customers to pay with a simple QR scan. The product runs on a system of smart contracts that effectively and efficiently manage counter-party risk, protecting both buyer and seller.

Supermoney are utilising blockchain to strategically focus on enterprise software solutions, loyalty program transformation and digital payments (using stable coins to facilitate faster, more secure transactions). From a loyalty perspective, their blockchain layer can link existing and new loyalty programs to support currency interchangeability, increasing the liquidity available to members.

A global juice chain are one of the first clients to sign. Their existing loyalty program will be linked to allow their members to transfer their points outside the program for redemption at other participating merchants, or transfer points in from other merchants to redeem on a free juice. The central tool for members is the Toucan App, which tokenises different loyalty currencies and supports the collection, trading and redemption of tokens across the retailer network.

I interviewed Supermoney *CEO Joel Smalley* about the company's vision and strategy.

'Our principle objective is to increase the value of the loyalty programs of our customers that we support. We see that this can be achieved by increasing visibility and liquidity. By tokenising points or miles on the same platform where we tokenise money as a regulated financial institution, we can subsequently display those loyalty tokens alongside their digital money in the wallet, making them visible at every POS transaction. More visibility inevitably means more utility, and liquidity increases as a result. In addition, customers of partners who elect to allow their loyalty tokens to be transferable can exchange those tokens for more desirable ones more easily under this approach. Ultimately, a DEX (decentralised exchange) can be integrated making it easier still for tokens to be traded, subject to necessary regulatory compliance, and even for the participation of market makers (liquidity providers). We expect at least 25% uplift in value as a result of increased liquidity and further benefit from superior insight into consumer behaviour and digital engagement.'

Having such significant companies embrace blockchain to solve real-world challenges is an exciting indicator that the technology certainly does have something valuable to offer.

CHAPTER 15
BLOCKCHAIN MARKETING

A PARALLEL INDUSTRY evolving alongside blockchain loyalty is the new field of blockchain marketing. From a loyalty perspective, blockchain marketing involves rewarding members with cryptocurrency or cryptotokens in exchange for their attention, brand advocacy and data insights, while giving them full control over their personal data which is stored in a secure digital wallet on the blockchain. The essence of blockchain marketing is marketers earning the member's permission to promote to them and access their personal data, with members able to earn a benefit for providing their attention and sharing their data.

A 2015 survey by Aimia and Columbia Business School identified consumers were growing increasingly weary of handing over their personal data but were willing to share if they received rewards.[34] The research showed 85 per cent of consumers globally wanted to know more information about the data collected by companies. A further 86 per cent wanted to exercise greater control over their data. 80 per cent of respondents said they would only give data to a few companies they trusted. Probably from real life experiences, 75 per cent were worried (and rightly so) that sharing data made them targets for marketing campaigns.

In 2018, the scandal surrounding Facebook and Cambridge Analytica's use of member data to influence the 2016 US presidential election led to a groundswell of public opposition against the use of personal data. One popular saying for these times is, 'If the product is free, then you're the product,'

---

34 http://marketingmag.ca/wp-content/uploads/2015/11/aimia.jpg

which certainly rings true when one considers how many companies use member data to boost their profits.

There is also the tightening up of personal data privacy and security rules, such as the implementation of the General Data Protection Regulation (GDPR) which was implemented 25th May 2018 in Europe and aims to 'protect all EU citizens from privacy and data breaches in an increasingly data-driven world that is (rapidly changing)'.[35] Data is now widely regarded as a valuable commodity and abuses of its use will be tolerated less and less.

All of this provides the perfect foundation for a new approach to data-driven, personalised marketing.

To illustrate how blockchain marketing may manifest within a cryptotoken loyalty program, consider a possible member lifecycle. The member joins the program with a simple registration process (name, email, password) and a secure digital blockchain wallet is created with the member holding the key. Over time, the member is invited to load their personal data into the secure wallet, for which they are rewarded with cryptotokens; date of birth, address, mobile number, links to social media profiles, gender, sexual orientation and so on. In parallel, the loyalty program collects the member's transaction data to understand the types of products they buy and where they shop. This may be from participating retailers, but the member might also be rewarded for scanning receipts from other major retailers. The member is also rewarded for filling in surveys to share their likes, dislikes, favourite brands and other information which can be used by the loyalty company to ascertain products and brands which will best appeal to them. The loyalty company can now work with reputable brands to deliver highly relevant and personalised promotions to the member. Should the member then choose to engage with those promotions, they would earn cryptotokens. They may be rewarded for viewing the promotion, but also for purchasing the product or service, and ideally for providing access to some or all of their data within their secure digital wallet so the brand can better understand them.

Compare this to all existing loyalty programs, where the loyalty company collects as much data as they can and does what they like with it (within the confines of data privacy and security legislation), with the member having no control and receiving no rewards.

---

35 https://www.eugdpr.org/

The premise of blockchain marketing is that if marketers know the value they can ascribe for a member's attention, advocacy or data, they'll be able to accurately decide what investment they should make in that member. This is similar to the approach used by companies such as Facebook with its advertising platform which allows marketers to set a fixed budget to reach a certain number of potential customers and accurately track the revenue outcome of the campaign activity. The stark difference is that the member is in control of their personal data (no Cambridge Analytica moments here) and is rewarded for their engagement.

From a company perspective, the true benefit of having access to an accurate data profile for a member is it allows them to better tailor their products, services, offers, rewards and marketing to meet their needs. For most companies, their member's personal data is isolated in the many different organisations that collected it, making an accumulated overall picture very difficult. The potential for blockchain marketing lies in incentivising the member to connect these disparate bits and pieces of information, then reward them further for adding additional information such as transaction data, personal biographies and likes, wants and needs.

When it comes to collecting transaction data, there is a clear distinction between capturing the amount the member spends and the actual products they purchased. If a loyalty company knows how much a member is spending at a particular retailer, that is incredibly useful in building a profile of that customer. If they know the specific products they purchased from that retailer, that is an exponentially more useful insight. For a company running their own loyalty program, collecting that transaction level data is relatively easy, but for a coalition program it's very hard. This is because the retailer rarely provides the product level data to the coalition operator, as only the total amount spent is required to calculate the amount of points earned.

To illustrate, if the member shows a history of purchasing KitKat chocolate bars and the loyalty program can collect this data, the member may be provided with the option to earn bonus cryptotokens for viewing a promotional offer from Nestle. Companies like Nestle often struggle to reach their customers directly because they sell through wholesalers and distributors to extensive retail networks, meaning the opportunity to build a direct relationship with a member is of high value to them. The member can indicate in their profile if they'd like to receive chocolate bar offers and they are willing to share their personal data profile to chocolate bar manufacturers in exchange for a cryptotoken reward. Nestle now has the opportunity to build a campaign using a much richer data set than they usually have access to and can target customers who are already consuming their product. They can incentivise the member to share the offer on social media, write positive reviews, fill in surveys and even forward the offer to family and friends. If executed correctly, Nestle now has an army of crypto ambassadors recruited to promote the KitKat brand. They may also be provided with the opportunity to target members who consume their competitors' products.

From a commercial perspective, this type of engagement approach has the potential to be incredibly cost effective, with the brand able to deliver one to one promotions to a member who has already indicated they want to receive offers and has provided access to their digital wallet to allow the brand to tailor an offer that specifically meets their needs. This reduces the need for costly ad services such as Google AdWords by creating a direct, desired link between the member and the company.

Blockchain marketing has the potential to be disruptive to the digital advertising industry, which is renowned for pushing advertisements to users which are irrelevant or based on out of date data. For example, I once bought a camping tent online and for weeks after the same company I bought the tent from pushed remarketing banner advertising at me on many of the websites I visited, trying to get me to buy the same tent. This was inefficient marketing spend for them and irritating for me.

Some of the blockchain marketing players which sit outside loyalty programs are taking a two-step approach; directly disrupting the digital advertising industry by blocking ads and trackers, while rewarding members for attending to ads they wish to receive. It is too early to say how much traction they will get in the market but it does have the feel of Netflix taking on free-to-air television.

Blockchain marketing fits perfectly within a blockchain loyalty program, for four reasons. Firstly, by registering with the program the member has already started down the path of providing their personal data and in a framework which makes sense to them because they've likely joined other loyalty programs before. Secondly, because earning cryptotokens is central to the design of the program, providing additional opportunities to earn by sharing data with preferred brands feels like a natural extension of the program, rather than the total program itself. Thirdly, the approach allows the loyalty company to position themselves as genuinely differentiated from existing loyalty programs which often subject their members to marketing assault and sell their data to third parties without the member being aware or being rewarded. A transparent, ethical marketing approach which gives members back control over their data is a sharp contrast to today's paradigm for which a sizeable consumer backlash is growing steam. It will also be virtually impossible for existing loyalty companies to change their approach, as their business operations are heavily dependent on the unhindered use of member data, meaning the differentiated position is also defensible. Fourthly, the approach has the potential to build into a valuable incremental revenue stream for the program, with brands eager to pay for the ability to send targeted marketing to members willing to hear from them. Consider a loyalty program with a base of 2 million members that can generate $10 per member incremental revenue per annum plus deliver additional cryptotoken rewards to the base.

While this new marketing approach fits neatly within loyalty program designs, at the time of writing there is yet to be a cryptotoken loyalty program who has adopted this approach, therefore from a loyalty perspective the concept is purely theoretical. That being said, there are a number of blockchain marketing companies operating independently to loyalty programs who can provide insight into different approaches a loyalty company can take. While it is still very early days for blockchain marketing, the space is fascinating and something worth watching closely as new business models evolve over the coming years. Let's take a look at a sample of the blockchain marketing players in existence today:

MyBron

www.mybron.com

Analysis by the team at MyBron identified that while there is a huge amount of data available about individuals, most of it is isolated in different organisations. They see an immense potential in connecting bits and pieces of information across data sources and contexts. MyBron incentivises users to connect these disparate data pools in exchange for Brons (the platform's cryptotoken), cash or exclusive offers. This clears a major hurdle in accessing consent from the user, as well as ensuring accurate matching of personally identifiable information (PII).

This is particularly relevant in the EU, Australia, Canada and other countries, where new privacy legislation regulations require individual data rights management and transparent consent mechanisms. The MyBron platform provides a flexible consent solution that can cover cross organisation data exchanges.

The MyBron platform allows users to link their social media accounts, submit validation documentations (similar to a KYC process) and input transaction data via their BronRewards platform. BronRewards incentivises users to scan and submit receipts from a wide variety of retailers in exchange for Bron points. Users can earn bonus Bron points for purchasing specific products, which are funded by the retailer or wholesaler. The points can be redeemed as cash or on gift cards.

The advantage of using blockchain is it allows MyBron to transparently store immutable and accessible cryptographic proofs of particular data snapshots or identity attributes. This is a key feature that will enable MyBron's data and identity marketplace to be decentralised and at the same time to maintain the integrity of the exchanged information. This is quite different to most loyalty programs which store the information in a central place and create potential targets for hackers. By decentralising this process, MyBron enables people to be more in control of what is shared and enables them to store their own personal information without damaging the integrity and the accuracy of the shared data.

Emma Poposka, CEO of MyBron, told me, 'The company does not intend to replace the third-party advertising networks, but its focus is to disrupt the traditional data brokerage model by empowering the individuals to capture the monetary value of their personal information. Unlike centralised data driven models where third parties hold contextual data on their customers without the intention for its cross-domain utilisation, MyBron enables its data wallet holders to use this information across contexts and to actively participate in the future of the data driven economy. Most importantly, the company is empowering users to have higher level of control over how their personal data (anonymised or including PII) is shared with third parties.'

Brave

www.brave.com

Brave provides a search engine browser which rewards users for their attention. Brave has a range of smarts. Ads and trackers are blocked, providing immediate privacy and ensuring the browser runs faster than Google and Safari as it doesn't need to download as much data. Brave state that the average large news site can contain as many as 70 ad trackers.

The core feature of Brave is their basic attention token (BAT) cryptotoken. Users can opt into their blockchain based digital advertising system, Brave Rewards, giving publishers a better deal and users a share of the ad revenue for their attention. Users can also donate BAT to their favourite websites and content creators to provide them with an alternative income from advertising revenue, thereby disrupting the industry. Users can also earn BAT by watching targeted ads.

Papyrus

www.papyrus.global

A decentralised advertising ecosystem, Papyrus identifies six major issues with the current digital advertising world: ads are irrelevant, annoying and invasive; trackers rob users of their privacy; targeting is unreliable and often uses out of date data; there are multiple intermediaries between the advertiser and the consumer, delivering little but increasing costs; up to 70 per cent of traffic paid for by advertisers is bots or fraud and the use of fiat currencies and banks to pay for global advertising generates high administrative and transactional costs.

Utilising a blockchain based approach, Papyrus delivers a range of benefits for users, publishers and advertisers. Users can control what advertising they receive and are compensated for their attention and sharing their data. Publishers can build new advertising approaches which reward attention and promote to a user base who are actively seeking personalised and relevant promotions. Advertisers are protected from bots and fraud, have a fully auditable transaction trail recorded on the blockchain and enjoy reduced costs with the elimination of intermediaries.

The Papyrus stack supports the development of decentralised applications (dApps), where the development is open source and evolves with consensus. Unlike other blockchain advertising projects that are focused on particular components of the digital advertising market like exchanges, marketplaces or browsers, Papyrus is an open ecosystem for all components, platforms and market players. Other projects can be integrated with Papyrus for mutual benefit.

Earn.com

www.earn.com

Earn.com describe themselves as 'the first token-based social network'. Members can earn digital currency by replying to emails and completing tasks. At the time of writing the main cryptocurrency they use is Bitcoin. Earn.com indicated they had plans to create their own cryptotoken which members will receive instead, but this is yet to come to fruition.

Registering for Earn.com requires the new member to provide relevant information to enable advertisers and sales staff to determine if they are a suitable target for their promotion. This includes a short biography, linking of social media profiles plus links to websites and email addresses. The idea is for the user to make themselves sound attractive, so they receive lots of requests for their attention. They can also set their price, starting at US$1, which can be cashed out into Bitcoin.

One clever feature is the ability for the member to link their account to their Gmail account. If anyone sends unsolicited emails to the account, the email is bounced and the sender is provided with the opportunity to pay for the member's attention via Earn.com.

From an advertiser's perspective, Earn.com allows for marketing campaigns to their mailing list and declare 60-80 per cent response rates, well above industry average. Companies can also use Earn.com to run surveys and even complete tasks.

In April 2018, Coinbase announced they were acquiring Earn.com for US$120m, indicating the massive potential of the blockchain marketing space.[36] They expanded the gamification elements of Earn.com onto Coinbase.com by providing members with the opportunity to earn crypto on Coinbase

---

36 https://techcrunch.com/2018/04/16/
coinbase-buys-earn-com-and-makes-ceo-balaji-srinivasan-its-first-cto/

by watching educational videos to learn about new coins and tokens, then earn them by answering skill-testing quizzes.

Universal Reward Protocol

www.rewardprotocol.com

Universal Reward Protocol (URP) aims to bridge the gap between offline and online and provide a platform for retailers to engage with customers directly. Their platform is built on the blockchain and powered by the URP token. Shoppers are rewarded with URP for sharing their personal data with a retailer, which could be data points such as a point of sale visit, their location, or their purchases. URP can then be redeemed with the retailer to take advantage of offers or promotions that have been tailored based on the data the shopper has already shared.

Retailers are required to purchase URP tokens in advance, which can generally be problematic for a cryptotoken which fluctuates in price, as it will be difficult to convince them to hold something today which can be worth less tomorrow.

The URP platform is supported by geolocation and machine learning, allowing the data to be analysed and profiled before being provided to retailers to support customisation of offers to members. More sensitive data (such as retailer-specific receipt data) will only be available to the retailer it originated from.

Max Savransky, Loyalty Director, Loyalty & Reward Co, spoke with Yves Benchimol, CEO & Co-Founder of Universal Reward Protocol.

'Universal Reward Protocol was launched and designed by Occi, a retail marketing technology company working with some of the largest retailer and brands worldwide, including Carrefour, Auchan and Nestlé,' said Benchimol. 'The Occi in-store behaviour intelligence layer, which is the result of three years of R&D, is already live in over 100,000 square meters of retail space in stores operated by some of the world's largest retailers, and will be the first URP-compliant oracle, focusing on in-store behaviour. While there are no retailers or brands publicly announced as part of the network yet, URP is backed by an impressive board of advisors, including Francois Poupard, former Head of Innovation at Auchan Retail and member of the Auchan founding family, and Samuel Baroukh, Head of e-Business at Nestlé France. Universal Reward

Protocol is currently on-boarding retailers and brands that want to be the first to use the technology and launch campaigns on the platform. 2019 will be one of the most important years for URP with the launch of the solution. We are targeting millions of shoppers and we hope to be able to announce such a number at the end of next year (2019).'

WOM Protocol

www.womprotocol.io

The power of word-of-mouth marketing has been acknowledged for some time. Blockchain marketing play WOM Protocol is attempting to build a disruptive marketing approach off the back of it.

Brands are forecast to spend $237 billion on advertising in 2019, yet their customers are likely to pay more attention to the 2.1 billion daily word-of-mouth product recommendations made by peers. Without mechanisms to measure these micro interactions, word-of-mouth recommendations have largely remained untracked and unrewarded.

Enter WOM Token. WOM claims to be the next generation of marketing which will record, track and reward word-of-mouth recommendations on the blockchain, creating a simpler, smarter and more transparent form of marketing for everyone.

The WOM Token aims to be an ecosystem for all content creators, consumers, curators, publishers and brands to engage with each other's content. Content creators share word-of-mouth recommendations online, and curators identify and validate the recommendations, earning WOM Tokens. Consumers engage with the WOM content and the creators earn WOM Tokens. Publishing platforms earn WOM Tokens as consumers engage with content on their platforms. Brands use WOM Tokens to access user-generated content, and smart contracts are dynamically generated between brands and content creators. Brands can then track word-of-mouth performance across their content creators' networks.

WOM have one Gen Z focused platform signed up so far called YEAY who have 170K registered users. WOM are creating 1 billion tokens and attempting to sell 350 million of them via ICO in early 2019 via a Dutch auction. If everything goes according to plan the maximum they will raise is US$350 million and the minimum will be US$10 million.

Will they succeed? According to Stacey Lyons, Marketing Director, Loyalty & Reward Co, 'The reason word-of-mouth is so effective is because the person giving the recommendation is usually a family member or friend who isn't being paid for their recommendation. As soon as a company monetises word-of-mouth this brings the credibility of the recommendation into question, making it immediately less effective. Take Instagram for example; it's very cluttered with both macro and micro-influencers from mummy-bloggers to beauty bloggers to Vloggers and more. The lines between advertising, sponsored content and paid PR are blurred as brands and influencer platforms alike have jumped on the bandwagon of monetising content. Now that consumers have caught on and the influencer market is flooded, the content has lost much of its impact and consumers have lost trust in the recommendations. Consumers always turn back to genuine word-of-mouth; a trusted, credible, personalised and unpaid source of information.'

TaTaTu

www.tatatu.com

TaTaTu made headlines in mid-2018 after raising a whopping US$575m via ICO to build a Netflix competitor which aims to reward viewers with TTU cryptotokens for watching premium content, with the cost of the tokens covered by advertising revenue. The TaTaTu platform isn't limited to movies but also offers music, sports and gaming videos.

New members are rewarded instantly. When signing up for TaTaTu they receive 50 TTU in their digital wallet which can be unlocked by viewing a further 50 TTU of content, effectively providing the member with 100 TTU. TaTaTu have a referral program, where members can invite family and friends to join and earn even more TTU. Members can also earn TTU for posting images, videos and more, although details of how this works aren't provided.

It's still early days for TaTaTu, but they also appear to be victims of the 2018-19 bear market. Debuting at 60 cents, the price of TTU rose to 80 cents only to plummet to a low of 1.8 cents in early-2019. It remains to be seen whether the US$575m they raised will be enough to generate sufficiently engrossing content and the critical mass of viewers to turn things around, however it is unlikely when their competitors have war chests of billions of dollars.

TapCoin by Hooch

www.tapcoin.net

TapCoin is already featured in Chapter 6 as a new cryptotoken loyalty program, however CEO & Co-founder Lin Dai views the company more as a blockchain marketing organisation. 'TAP plans on decentralising the monetisation of data by giving the control back to the consumers,' said Dai. 'Consumers can decide which brands to grant permission to their data and store their permission in a smart contract. Permitted brands will be able to access data and insights by directly depositing TAP Coin into consumer's TAP wallet, and encourage consumers to take an action such as redeem the TAP Coin for a free product or $x off a purchase. Trusted publishers and media companies can serve as data delegates and help consumers store and share their data on the TAP network and receive a percentage of the brand advertising revenue. It's a win for all parties, rather than today's advertising ecosystem where centralized publishers such as Facebook use consumer data for targeting and keep 100 per cent of the advertising revenue.'

Hooch has some pretty big name brands like Bacardi and Paramount currently using their app to advertise, but their new blockchain marketing approach via TapCoin clearly has the potential to optimise the advertiser's budget as well as the user experience.

Blockchain marketing also fits neatly into other major advances in marketing technology, such as augmented reality (AR) and virtual reality (VR). Imagine this AR future: you're walking down the street wearing a pair of smart glasses or a discrete holoprojector. As you progress, a coin symbol pops up on the screen, a small 3D image hovering over a store selling running shoes. You tap the coin to view an offer which says '20 per cent off any transaction', plus you've just earned bonus cryptotokens for your attention. You tap the 'Tell Them I'm Coming' button and head to the store. A packet of your relevant personal data is sent ahead to the store and when you arrive a minute later, someone is there to greet you at the door. Their tablet has received your packet of personal data to tell them your name, shoe size and purchase history so they can tailor your shopping experience to perfectly meet your needs. You choose a pair of shoes and buy them with cryptotokens you've earned from the loyalty program, with the entire transaction processed via your glasses or holo device.

The shoes you buy have LOOMIA fabric woven in and when you leave the shop you're invited to store and share your usage data to earn more bonus cryptotokens. You're also invited to connect to your health insurance fund's rewards app to earn bonus cryptotokens for taking a minimum number of steps each day. A year later when you've taken a large number of steps in your new shoes, you receive marketing from a small range of your favourite shoe companies for your next purchase with discount offers and bonus cryptotokens. In the future, the centre of the universe is you and you really do know how much you're worth.

VR offers even more exciting potential, with new digital worlds offering a plethora of opportunities for blockchain marketing. One entrant to this market is Gaze Coin, which has developed a VR application that rewards users for how long they hold their attention on a particular feature of the game. Their motto is 'Get Paid to Gaze', which is a brand new way for users to engage with a new technology.

Gaze Coin identified a clear problem with early VR/AR applications, which were designed to get their users to click, tap and hit play, actions borrowed from gaming consoles and PC. Their breakthrough came by realising that VR is more about seeing, touching and experiencing and that the monetisation of VR and AR was being constrained by old school media models. Gaze Coin allows audiences to trigger content by looking in the direction of the content and holding their attention. The model calculates the amount of time users spend immersed inside specific content and creates a micropayment that charges advertisers for that time, pays the content owner and rewards the users for consuming the content.

An example of how Gaze Coin can be applied is a DJ wanting to promote their upcoming tour. They can create their own VR world where fans can enter a virtual dance party and listen to the DJ's latest set. The more time they spend at the party watching the DJ, the more Gaze Coins they earn (or even DJ coins if the DJ wishes to brand the tokens as their own), which they can use to get a discount or a free ticket when the DJ comes to town. Thus, fans are rewarded for their attention in a virtual world with an opportunity to party in the real world. The lines between digital and reality are rapidly fading.

CHAPTER 16

IT'S ALL ABOUT DECENTRALISATION

In March 2018, I was invited to present my blockchain loyalty research paper at the International Symposium on Foundations and Applications of Big Data Analytics (FAB) 2018, a blockchain symposium at University of Southern California partly organised by Microsoft (the paper can be found in the Appendix). An earlier version of the paper was reviewed and critiqued by the panel. One piece of feedback received was of particular interest. 'One of the main reasons to use blockchain and cryptocurrency is to have a decentralised trust authority. The programme implemented just acts as a centralized conduit to cryptocurrency so the main novelty of using blockchain technology is not realized here.'

The central premise of the UNSW research and this book has been that the fundamental structure of a loyalty program has stood the test of time and that one of the main opportunities that blockchain delivers is the ability to replace points and miles with a cryptotoken to solve some of the inherent limitations. The feedback from the reviewer was that this doesn't go far enough and not only should the value of the currency be decentralised but the entire program should be decentralised.

This kicked off a new round of investigation and exploration as I tackled the question of whether this was even possible and if so, whether it could deliver additional benefits versus a centralised loyalty program with a decentralised currency.

Firstly, it's important to clarify what is meant by a decentralised program.

In a paper titled *The General Theory of Decentralized Applications, dApps*, by Johnston et al[37], a decentralised application must meet four key criteria:

1. It must be completely open source, operate autonomously and with no entity controlling the token majority. Changes to the application must be adopted by consensus.

2. Data must be cryptographically stored in a distributed blockchain to avoid central failure points.

3. The application must use a cryptographic token for access to the application and as a reward to network supporters.

4. The application must generate tokens according to an algorithm that values contributions to the system.

For a loyalty program using a hybrid solution comprised of a non-blockchain loyalty platform connected to a blockchain platform, the application is clearly not decentralised. While a cryptotoken is used to reward supporters (for their engagement) and the application generates cryptotokens that value contributions to the system (such as retail partner transactions), the loyalty program code isn't open source, it doesn't operate autonomously, changes don't require consensus and for the most part the data doesn't need to be stored on a blockchain. There is also an entity controlling the cryptotoken majority.

So, what might a fully decentralised blockchain loyalty program look like? This would involve development of the platform and running of the program to be jointly managed by a disparate group of individuals which evolve the program by consensus. Is this even feasible for a loyalty program, which requires extensive non-development support, such as retail partner negotiations and invoicing, marketing and member support to function at a basic level? And what additional benefits would it deliver?

According to Vitalik Buterin,[38] developer of Ethereum, there are three arguments for why decentralisation is useful:

---

37 Johnston, D., Yilmaz, S.O., Kandah, J., Bentenitis, N., Hashemi, F., Gross, R., Wilkinson, S. & Mason, S., 'The General Theory of Decentralized Applications, Dapps', 2015

38 https://medium.com/@VitalikButerin/the-meaning-of-decentralization-a0c92b76a274

1. Fault tolerance: decentralised systems are less likely to fail accidentally because they rely on many separate components that are not likely (to fail simultaneously).

2. Attack resistance: decentralised systems are more expensive to attack and destroy or manipulate because they lack sensitive central points that can be attacked at much lower cost than the economic size of the surrounding system.

3. Collusion resistance: it is much harder for participants in decentralised systems to collude to act in ways that benefit them at the expense of other participants, whereas the leaderships of corporations and governments collude in ways that benefit themselves but harm less well coordinated citizens, customers, employees and the general public all the time.

The first two points make some sense from a system security point of view but there are other ways to protect core systems from attack which don't require a decentralised approach.

The third point is much more relevant for a modern loyalty program. If we consider that major coalition loyalty programs have actively devalued their own currencies in order to boost their profits at the expense of their highly loyal members, we can see an argument for collusion resistance. Of course, this issue is already solved by replacing points and miles with a cryptotoken, as the value of the cryptotoken is decentralised. Another technique coalition loyalty programs have used to boost profits is adjusting their rules to increase the number of points which expire. For example, one major frequent flyer program's terms and conditions stated members needed to earn at least one point or redeem at least one point every 24 months for all the points in the member's account to remain active. With an increase in program engagement due to a rise in popularity for their program, the amount of points expiring each year started to fall, so they reduced the number of months of inactivity from 24 to 18 months to boost their point expiry percentage to maintain their profitability. Under a decentralised loyalty program structure this type of rule change would require consensus. Once again this is already solved automatically by using a cryptotoken, as they never expire and therefore don't require expiry rules. Thus, even the concept of collusion resistance doesn't appear to be sufficient to argue for a fully decentralised loyalty program over a hybrid program.

One key argument put forward by industry commentators on the benefits decentralisation through blockchain can bring to the loyalty industry is the issue of fragmentation. The premise of the argument is that a single individual can belong to many loyalty programs, each with their own currencies, rules and restrictions. This has led to a situation where tens of billions of dollars of points and miles are held in different accounts but at such a low value they cannot be used. By connecting all of these programs to a single blockchain program, members would be able to transfer them into a single token and bundle the value together, thereby unlocking the value and making loyalty great again. Businesses will be delighted by this advancement, the argument stresses, because it will remove a massive liability from their accounts.

This is challenging. While some companies may embrace this opportunity (such as the current and future clients of Momentum Protocol and Digitalbits), many others won't want to. If they wished to allow their members to pool their points or miles earned from multiple loyalty programs, they could have simply joined one of the many dominant coalition programs which have existed since the 1980s. They haven't, either because they wish to keep the points and miles spend within their own ecosystem (thus ensuring the revenue doesn't leave their walled garden) or because competitors have already joined the coalition program and locked them out with exclusivity provisions in the partner contract. In the case of the second point, they wouldn't want their members transferring their points or miles into tokens and pooling it with reward currency earned from their competitors, as there's no competitive advantage for doing so.

With respect to balance sheet liability, it needs to be stated that this isn't an issue for most well-structured loyalty programs. An often cited, but in my opinion highly misleading, *Harvard Business Review* article by Kowalewski et al[39] states 'Blockchain could help relieve a large balance-sheet liability that many in the industry are facing... Loyalty programs have long relied on cobranded cards and partnerships to sell points and generate incremental revenue. But the number of airline seats and hotel rooms available for redemption in recent years has been limited by near-record occupancy and load factors. The result has been a growing volume of unredeemed points, which new

---

39 https://hbr.org/2017/03/blockchain-will-transform-customer-loyalty-programs

accounting standards have turned into a headache: Revenue attributable to the value of loyalty points must be deferred until the miles are redeemed.'

This argument is naive at best. The accounting standards governing points and miles based loyalty programs have been around for decades and they aren't a headache and are relatively simple. When points or miles are awarded to a member, the loyalty program must defer enough revenue to a separate account to cover the cost of the future liability. As stated earlier, some programs, such as the major frequent flyer programs, are carrying liabilities of several billion dollars. Do they care? Not in the slightest. In fact, most of them have specific strategies to grow the liability over time. They wish for the number of points or miles earned each year to be slightly higher than the amount redeemed. By following their strict accounting processes, they have enough funds to cover the liability, therefore it isn't an issue. In the meantime, they earn interest on the deferred revenue which adds to the program profitability.

In the event that a loyalty program allows for their currency to be redeemed on products outside their own ecosystem, they generally tend to structure their rewards range so the best value for members is to redeem on their own products (such as flights), with very poor value provided for third party products (such as gift cards and iPhones) in order to maintain most of the spend within their business. Some programs also allow their currency to be transferred into the currency of another program. When this happens, the conversion rates are generally very poor to dissuade members from doing it. To argue that a majority of companies will support a unifying blockchain loyalty approach which allows members to transfer their points or miles out of their ecosystem and maintain the value is pure fantasy.

While I am not opposed to the idea of a fully decentralised blockchain loyalty program and continue to explore its potential, I'm yet to identify a meaningful benefit which cannot be delivered by a hybrid solution which utilises a standard loyalty design with a cryptotoken instead of points and miles. I leave this discussion open for debate in the hope I may discover something which has thus far eluded me and will likely revisit the topic in future editions of *Blockchain Loyalty* and on *www.blockchainloyalty.io*.

CONCLUSION

LOYALTY PROGRAMS HAVE stood the test of time. They have been successfully generating repeat business for centuries and will continue to do so for centuries to come. The core problem with today's loyalty industry is a lack of value, excessive saturation and homogenisation and unrelenting marketing assault. The industry is certainly ripe for disruption and blockchain provides one of the biggest opportunities to do so since the invention of the frequent flyer program in the early 1980s.

While cryptocurrencies and cryptotokens solve many of the shortcomings of points and miles, they also have challenges, including the stigma associated with their early usage to buy drugs and launder money, the wild value fluctuations, the different approaches required for marketing and the uncertainty in different countries regarding tax and legal regulations.

The truly ground-breaking innovation with blockchain in loyalty is happening at the enterprise level, where companies such as Loyyal are streamlining legacy processes which were designed in the 1980's, while opening up the potential for vast global networks of loyalty players.

As with everything which manifests in a capitalistic environment, the market will decide. Enough money was raised during the past few years to launch a large number of exciting start-ups that are attempting to disrupt a wide range of industries using cryptocurrency loyalty, blockchain gamification, blockchain marketing and enterprise blockchain loyalty solutions.

The invention of blockchain provides a wonderful opportunity to reinvent everything to do with loyalty, not least the invasive marketing habits which have become a mainstream negative consequence of joining a program. Placing the member where they belong, in the centre of the company's universe, allows for a resetting of the communication approach to one where the member is rewarded for their attention, not ambushed for it.

I am extremely positive for the future of the loyalty industry. With the introduction of new currencies, new marketing models and, the opportunity exists for everything to be cast anew and the member rewarded for the one thing programs are designed to generate - loyalty.

This area is very new and future editions of this book will be able to provide a much more comprehensive insight into the optimal application of blockchain loyalty once companies around the world have had time to gain traction, build momentum and work through the regulatory environment of the countries in which they operate.

Visit *www.blockchainloyalty.io* for regular industry updates and to provide feedback on Blockchain Loyalty. As with any new industry innovation, discussion and debate are critical to advancement and are strongly encouraged.

EXPERIENCES FROM THE FIELD: UNIFY REWARDS - A CRYPTOCURRENCY LOYALTY PROGRAM

Philip Shelper
Chief Executive Officer
LoyaltyX
Sydney, Australia
philip.shelper@loyaltyx.co

Andrew Lowe
Managing Director
PicoLabs
Sydney, Australia
andrew.l@picolabs.co

Salil S. Kanhere
School of Computer Science and Engineering
UNSW Sydney
Sydney, Australia
salil.kanhere@unsw.edu.au

ABSTRACT

The emergence of cryptocurrencies has created new opportunities for loyalty programs. In this paper, we present a proof-of-concept cryptocurrency loyalty program called Unify Rewards where participants earned Ether cryptocurrency by making purchases at participating retailers. We outline the experiences gained from conducting a field trial of the program with student and staff at UNSW Sydney. The results from the trial which included 177 participants suggests that cryptocurrency is a viable alternative to loyalty miles and points.

Categories and Subject Descriptors

K.4.4 [**Computers and Society**]: Electronic Commerce – *cybercash, digital cash, distributed commercial transactions, payment schemes.*

Keywords

Cryptocurrency, Ether, Blockchain, Blockchain Loyalty, Loyalty Program, Field Trial

1. INTRODUCTION

The invention of blockchain and cryptocurrencies has inadvertently created an opportunity for a paradigm shift in loyalty program design.

From the 1980's until present day, the dominant currencies within loyalty programs have been 'miles' or 'points'. This has been adopted by major coalition programs generating billions of dollars of revenue per annum, as well as individual retailers with niche programs, and everything in between. Creating a currency which can be controlled by an organization has become a very useful tool for customer engagement, and a viable alternative to product discounting.

Even so, miles and points have limitations which restrict their attractiveness to consumers; they expire, they can only be redeemed on a limited reward range, and the value can be manipulated by the issuer to increase profits.

With the rise of Bitcoin [1] and other cryptocurrencies, a number of specialized Blockchain loyalty companies have been created. These include Gatcoin, CampusCoin, Nexxus Rewards, LoyalCoin and EzToken. These companies tend to follow a similar business design; create a new cryptocurrency, raise funding via an Initial Coin Offering, build a loyalty platform, float the cryptocurrency on an exchange so it can be traded, then seek merchants and members to generate demand for the cryptocurrency to drive up the value. Many of the companies have positioned their approach as one which will disrupt the loyalty industry.

With millions of dollars being invested in these companies, numerous questions arise; Is cryptocurrency a viable alternative for miles or points in a modern loyalty program? Would offering cryptocurrency to members drive deeper engagement with the program than offering miles or points? Does a cryptocurrency-based loyalty program have the potential to disrupt the loyalty industry? Would consumers view cryptocurrencies as any different to cash?

To answer these questions, we designed a proof-of-concept loyalty program called Unify Rewards and tested it in the real-world on the UNSW Sydney campus. Students and staff of UNSW Sydney were invited to join the program, where by transacting with a choice of 12 campus retailers, they earned Ether cryptocurrency over a 5-week period.

The results from the trial which included over 170 participants indicate cryptocurrencies can indeed act as an effective substitute for loyalty points, with evidence indicating they have the potential to drive much deeper engagement with a program by solving a number of the limitations inherent in miles and points-based programs.

The rest of the paper is organized as follows. Section 2 provides a history of loyalty programs. Section 3 presents motivating arguments for using cryptocurrencies in loyalty programs. Section 5 presents an overview of the Unify Rewards systems. Section 5 summarizes the evaluations from our field trial. Section 6 makes concluding remarks.

2. BACKGROUND

Egyptologists have uncovered evidence that ancient Egyptians practiced a type of reward program similar to modern frequent flyer programs, including status tiers and the ability to redeem on a wider variety of rewards. In [2], Professor Barry Kemp reminds us that for much of the Pharaoh's thousands of years of rule, they didn't have money. It simply wasn't invented yet. Instead they used a system much more aligned to a modern loyalty program. Citizens, conscripted workers and slaves alike were all awarded commodity tokens (similar to loyalty points or cryptocurrencies) for their work and temple time. The most common were beer and bread tokens. The tokens were made from wood, then plastered over and painted, and shaped like a jug of beer or a loaf of bread.

The tokens could also be exchanged for things other than bread and beer. Those high up enough to earn surplus tokens could redeem them on something else, just in the same way that frequent flyer members with lots of points can redeem them both on flights and on non-flight rewards such as iPads, KitchenAid mixers and Gucci handbags.

A more modern history of loyalty program currencies can be traced to the 1700's. In 1793, a U.S. merchant began rewarding customers with copper tokens, which could be used for future purchases, thereby generating repeat visits, a core focus of loyalty program design. The idea was quickly replicated by other merchants [3].

The Grand Union Tea Company was formed in 1872 in Pennsylvania. The owners chose to side-step merchants and sell their product directly to consumers, starting with door-to-door sales. They began rewarding customers with tickets which could be collected and redeemed for a wide selection of products from the company's Catalog of Premiums, which included such rewards as an Oak Roman Chair (100 tickets), lace curtains (120 tickets a pair), Ormolu clock (300 tickets), and dinner set Berlin 1903 (440 tickets). [4]

In the 1890's, marketers turned to the physical stamp to reward loyal customers. Customers earned stamps when making purchases and were encouraged to stick them into collecting books. The books could be exchanged for a wide range of rewards. The Sperry and Hutchinson Company came to dominate this type of loyalty currency approach with their S&H Green Stamps, which could be earned from a range of different merchants in an early form of coalition program. The program was so popular S&H even opened their own redemption center stores where merchandise could be purchased using books. At one point S&H claimed they were distributing 3 times as many Green Stamps as the US Postal Service was distributing postal stamps. [5]

The 1980's marked the beginning of the end for stamps when American Airlines launched the world's first currency-based frequent flyer program. They introduced a new currency, *miles*, which corresponded to how many miles a member had flown. Brought on by increasing competition with the deregulation of the US airline industry in 1978, the American Airlines AAdvantage program was soon followed by similar plays from United Airlines, TWA and Delta Airlines. Other airlines around the world quickly replicated. In 1987, Southwest Airlines launched a program which awarded *'points'* to members for trips flown, irrespective of the number of miles. Soon after the launch of the early programs, hotel and car rental companies partnered with the airlines and started offering miles and points as a way to grow their market share of the lucrative business travelers and high-value leisure travelers. The first roots of the modern, multi-billion dollar coalition loyalty programs took hold [6].

With the rapid expansion of the frequent flyer programs and their new currencies, other retailers soon replicated their approach, and miles & points became the dominant loyalty-program currencies.

3. MOTIVATION

From a loyalty perspective, the invention of cryptocurrencies is particularly interesting as it provides a viable alternative to miles or points.

Despite their dominance, miles and points (and indeed many of their predecessors) have limitations which restrict their attractiveness to consumers; (a) their lack of utility, (b) their ability to expire and (c) their systematic devaluation by loyalty program operators:

- Limited Utility: Most loyalty programs only allow miles/points to be used within their eco-system. This might be on flights, upgrades, an online store, retail vouchers or other company-specific discounts. One of the key frustrations for many frequent flyer program members is the lack of availability of flights when they try to use their miles/points i.e. they have miles/points but there are no flights they can spend them on. A cryptocurrency doesn't have any of these limitations. It can be bought, sold, transferred, gifted, sent overseas or converted into other cryptocurrencies or fiat currencies.

- Points Expiry: Members who aren't highly-engaged with a program can lose value when their miles or points expire. This might be because the miles/points aged and expired (e.g. points expire 2 years from issuance) or because there was no account activity for a specified period (e.g. points expire if there is no activity on the account for an 18-month period). Major coalition programs use actuaries to deliberately manage the program to maintain a set expiry rate in order to maximise their program profitability. Cryptocurrencies avoid these issues; they don't expire.

- Systematic Devaluation: A major airline loyalty program launched an online store in 2008 which allowed members to redeem points for merchandise and gift cards. This included a $100 gift card for a popular department store for 13,500 points. Today, the same $100 gift card costs 16,800 points. The value of the points has been devalued by the airline to extract more profit from the program. Cryptocurrencies doesn't reduce in value as they become more popular. Market forces of supply & demand support a value increase as the cryptocurrency becomes more desired, ensuring the value accumulated by members also increases.

Based on the benefits which cryptocurrencies provide compared to miles and points, we identified the potential for cryptocurrencies to deliver a more satisfying experience.

The other aspect of cryptocurrencies, the sometimes wild price fluctuations, were also identified as being a compelling characteristic of cryptocurrencies compared to miles/points. While the value of miles/points generally tend to remain static (ignoring any devaluation events), the value of cryptocurrencies such as bitcoin and Ether can fluctuate 25% in a single day. We were interested to understand whether this would be a significant element in affecting the member's overall engagement with the program. We also identified this as a key differentiator to earning cash.

4. UNIFY REWARDS: OVERVIEW OF THE SYSTEM AND THE FIELD TRIAL

It was agreed the best way to conduct the research was by creating a live-market loyalty program called Unify Rewards which mimicked other loyalty programs, with the main difference being the reward currency would be a popular cryptocurrency; Ether. The trial ran from 13th October 2017 to 18th November 2017.

4.1 MERCHANTS

Twelve retailers at UNSW Sydney were enrolled as program merchants. With an actual loyalty program the merchant would be required to cover the cost of the reward currency provided to the participant, however for the purposes of the trial merchants were not required to contribute anything, with all currency costs covered by the project budget.

4.2 SYSTEM

We recruited two loyalty companies to build the solution; Pico and Loyalty Corp. Pico provide a proprietary cloud-based point-of-sale data collection solution. Honeywell scanners connected to Pico units (comprised of a Raspberry Pi) were placed near the point-of-sale system at each merchant. When the participant scanned a unique barcode from their mobile device, the Pico unit sent the participant ID with a date & time stamp into the cloud, where it was captured and sent via API to Loyalty Corp's platform.

Loyalty Corp provided the front-end and back-end loyalty platform solution. A web app was developed which allowed students & staff to register for the program. Once registered they could access an account which showed their barcode, their account balance, plus it allowed them to process a redemption transaction. The back-end captured the transaction event from Pico and loaded the data into the participant's account real-time, allowing them to see that they had successfully earned for their scan.

When 10 stamps were collected, the Loyalty Corp platform purchased Ether from the Ethereum blockchain and added it to the member's account. Figure 1 depicts the system and outlines the various steps described above.

4.3 PARTICIPATION ENROLMENT

The enrolment process was more extensive than most loyalty programs due to a range of additional requirements provided by the University's Ethics Committee.

As the participants were agreeing to a formal research project, they were not only required to provide standard loyalty program registration details (name, email address and password) but they also were required to agree to the university's extensive research participation criteria.

This may have dissuaded some students and staff from completing the registration process, however there is no evidence to support this.

4.4 EARNING CRYPTOCURRENCY

To earn Ether cryptocurrency, participants conducted a transaction at any of the merchants. Irrespective of the size of the transaction, the participants were permitted to scan their unique barcode via the dedicated scanner. Scanning earned them one digital stamp, which appeared in their web app account. Participants were permitted to earn up to 5 stamps per day. When the participant earned 10 stamps, the stamps automatically converted into Ether.

To ensure participants had the experience of owning Ether for as long as possible, a $5 Ether join bonus was provided to them at the beginning of the trial.

At the start of the project participants could earn $5 of Ether for 10 stamps. From the second week, this was increased to $10 of Ether for a marketing exercise (Double Ether Week) but ended up being maintained for the remainder of the trial.

When a participant earned their Ether allocation, part of an Ether was provided to them, with the amount calculated on the dollar amount they had earned ($10) and the price of Ether at the time of the earn event.

Participants were not required to create a separate Ether cryptocurrency wallet, as their Ether balance was held for them in trust within their loyalty account.

4.5 REDEMPTION

Participants had a range of options for redeeming their Ether balance. Throughout the trial they could:

- Cash their balance into an e-wallet. The Ether was sold at the actual market rate, and they funds were transferred into an e-wallet held within the web app. They could use the balance to access a discount on a range of popular gift cards.

- Cash their balance into a bank account. The Ether was sold at the actual market rate, and they funds were transferred into the participants nominated bank account.

- Transfer their balance to another participant, simply by using the recipient's registered email address.

At the end of the trial, participants were also provided with the opportunity to transfer their balance to their personal Ether Wallet. For those participants who didn't have a wallet, instructions were provided on how to create one.

4.6 MARKETING

As with any consumer loyalty program, a range of marketing communications were sent to participants during the trial to educate them and stimulate engagement with the program.

The ambition of the marketing strategy was to persuade as many participants as possible to accumulate at least ten stamps, earning an Ether payout of $5 to $10, in order to provide them with a significant enough experience to be able to meaningfully complete a survey at the end of the trial.

Marketing campaigns during the trial included:

- Welcome email: Provided participants with relevant information to educate them about the essential elements of the trial.

- $5 Ether join bonus: Provided participants with an Ether balance early in the program so they could explore the concept of cryptocurrency ownership more deeply given the trial time constraints.

- Win One Ether competition: Participants received one entry for each stamp they earned to encourage early swiping and engagement.

- Cool earn tips from a member: An educational email detailing insight from a participant on how to maximise stamps earned.

- Double Ether week: Designed to drive ongoing engagement with the program by increasing the prize for earning ten stamps.

- Price of Ether: an educational email detailing the price fluctuations of Ether, designed to generate interest amongst participants in following the price changes.

- Last week of Unify Rewards: Designed to communicate the end date of the program and encourage participants to make the most of their last few days to scan and earn.

- Survey: An invitation to complete the research survey for the program.

5. EVALUATIONS

In the following we present results from the field trial.

5.1 REGISTRATION

177 participants registered for the program. Due to delays with the Ethics Committee approval process, the two-week registration window was reduced to 3 days, which included a weekend (thus one business day). Despite the severe reduction in time, the authors were very happy with the high number of registrations.

5.2 PARTICIPATION

Scans were strongest in the first two weeks of the trial. They dropped off during exam period as many students were not on campus during that period (or frequented campus less regularly).

The spread of total stamps earned during the trial was as follows.

- 21% of participants earn 0 stamps (registered but didn't engage further)

- 18% earned 1-9 stamps

- 61% earned 10 stamps or more (achieving the project target for engagement as it allowed them to earn at least one allocation of Ether)

Even more encouragingly, 18% earned 20 stamps or more.

This is a very high engagement rate for a loyalty program compared to industry averages. By comparison, two major loyalty programs in Australia show member engagement rates of 57% (a major supermarket chain) and 37% (a major liquor chain).

5.3 MARKETING ENGAGEMENT

Figure 1: EDM Response

Engagement with the marketing communications was consistently high. The minimum open rate for Electronic Direct Mail (EDM) was 48.3% and the maximum was 72.7%, well above the industry average for loyalty programs which sits at around 20%. Figure 2 illustrates EDM open rates over the trial period. During the trial period, just two participants unsubscribed from communications. This indicates strong engagement with the program by a majority of participants.

5.4 REDEMPTION BEHAVIOR

With respect to redemption behaviour:

- 67% of participants chose to transfer their Ether to their personal Ether Wallet

- 29% of participants chose to cash in their Ether for a deposit into their bank account

- 4% of participants chose to cash in their Ether to use for a gift card
- 0% of participants transferred their ETH allocation to another participant

The outcome indicates a strong propensity from a majority of participants to hold their Ether for speculative purposes, an advantage cryptocurrencies have over loyalty points, and one which the survey results identified as being particularly attractive to members. This provides a sharp contract to a program where they might earn cash, which has little speculative potential for the average consumer.

5.5 SURVEY RESULTS

72 participants completed the post-project qualitative survey. Participants who didn't earn any stamps were not invited to fill in the survey, as it was felt they had not engaged with the program, therefore wouldn't have sufficient insight to provide a meaningful opinion.

Participants indicated they were generally well-exposed to points-based loyalty programs, with only one respondent indicating they didn't belong to any program. This meant participants had sufficient insight to compare a points program to a cryptocurrency program.

Overwhelmingly the results indicate participants found a cryptocurrency-based program to be more engaging than a points-based program. Respondents reported the following:

- They found Unify Rewards to be more rewarding than their favourite loyalty program (7.58 vs 6.04/10)

- They felt Unify Rewards was more motivating in influencing them to spend their money with participating merchants than their favourite loyalty program (7.80 vs 5.98/10)

- They reported both Unify Rewards and their favourite loyalty program had motivated them to modify the way they spent money to maximise their loyalty currency earn (83% for Unify Rewards vs 80% for their favourite loyalty program). This is strong result for both approaches and provides evidence loyalty programs can be effective in influencing consumer spend behaviour.

- They provided a higher Net Promoter Score for Unify Rewards than their favourite loyalty program (8.53 vs 5.72/10)

- 59% spent more money on campus during the trial period. A further 41% reporting spending the same.

- 86% felt Unify Rewards was more appealing than their favourite loyalty program, and 11% felt it was just as appealing.

Some of the positive reasons cited included:

- The concept is interesting since the value can fluctuate.

- There's a bit of mystery about Ether - it's a bit of a wild card so there's an element of speculation and potential that makes it exciting. But it's not a guaranteed thing.

- Cryptocurrency is cool, exposed me to it

- Cryptocurrency is a very exciting currency as it fluctuates and you never know what to expect the next day. It might go up, or go down, and it is a great experience to learn about how it works and what influences it.

- The possibility of growing value and ability to cash out when you like is very attract.

- More appealing because of the tangible dollar value of the ether as opposed to less tangible points

- Ether feels like you're getting money rather than "points". When Ether was low, I was incentivised to spend and reach the next 10 before Ether spiked.

Some of the negative reasons cited included:

- There is too much fluctuation with cryptocurrency.

- It was an interesting reward, but also felt to be of little difference to cash.

Further analysis of the survey data identified evidence to suggest surveyed participants who were less satisfied with the level of reward from existing loyalty schemes were more likely to find earning Ether more appealing.

While the research was focused on members and not merchants, the verbal feedback from merchants was positive due to the increase in spend by members seeking to earn more Ether. This would only increase with scale.

6. CONCLUSIONS AND FUTURE WORK

The evolution of currencies in loyalty programs shows a long and varied history. Tokens, tickets, stamps, miles and points have all been invested as a device to stimulate loyalty from worshippers and customers, often with great success. They also carry limitations, including limited utility, expiry and devaluation characteristics. With miles & points dominating as the main loyalty currency for over 35 years, it would not be unusual in the history of loyalty for them to be replaced by a new currency design.

Our world-first field trial has shown cryptocurrencies have the potential to be that new currency. The research demonstrated offering Ether as an alternative to miles/points generated very strong engagement with the Unify Rewards program, with 86% of survey respondents reporting they found it to be more appealing that the points they earn from their favorite loyalty program.

While some members drew comparisons with cash, the overwhelming opinion from members indicated they felt cryptocurrencies were more exciting and desirable due to value fluctuations ('you never know what to expect the next day') and the potential for a significant future value increase ('there's an element of speculation and potential that makes it exciting'). It is also telling that 67% of participants chose to hold (or HODL) their Ether rather than cash it in. In that sense, we argue cryptocurrencies injects a unique and highly-engaging gamified element into the program which is absent from points & miles programs, and cash programs.

Some merchants may not appreciate that the cryptocurrencies earned within the program can be transferred externally, rather than reinvested with them. This issue can be offset via quality customer experience design in two ways; firstly, by making it really easy and worthwhile to spend with the merchant, and secondly by allowing the member to transfer other cryptocurrencies into the eco-system to be easily spent with the merchant.

Further research is required to explore the potential of cryptocurrencies in future loyalty program design. The Unify Rewards earn approach, where 10 stamps were required to earn $10 Ether, was simplistic and didn't take into account the amount of spend made in each transaction. A new research project which ties the amount of cryptocurrency earned to the amount spent would provide an additional insight; whether cryptocurrency loyalty programs are more effective in driving higher transactional spend than miles & points-based programs.

Another aspect which was not possible to measure with Unify Rewards is the effectiveness of a new cryptocurrency in driving engagement behavior. While some companies may choose to utilize existing, popular cryptocurrencies such as Bitcoin and Ether, the bigger opportunity is for a company to create an original cryptocurrency with full control over the amount created and how it is distributed. This would likely involve a greater investment to build awareness of, and desire for, the currency, and would require a longer timeframe to determine any results.

Our research indicated cryptocurrencies do have a key role to play in the future design of loyalty programs, and companies around the world already running a miles/points-based program, or considering implementing one, should seriously consider cryptocurrencies as a viable alternative.

7. REFERENCES

[1]   S. Nakamoto, "Bitcoin: A Peer-to-Peer Electronic Cash System," 2009. [Online]. Available: https://bitcoin.org/bitcoin.pdf. [Accessed 11 12 2017].

[2]   B. J. Kemp, Ancient Egypt: Anatomy of a Civilization, 2nd Edition ed., Routledge, 2006.

[3]   C. T. &. B. Innovator, "The Loyalty Evolution," New York, 2016.

[4]   G. U. T. Company, Grand Union Tea Company - Catalogue of Premiums 1903, 1903.

[5]   S. &. Hutchinson, S & H Green Stamps Ideabook of Distinguished Merchandise: 70th Anniversary Edition, 1966.

[6]   R. Petersen, "History of Frequent Flyers Program," 2001. [Online]. Available: http://www.webflyer.com/company/press_room/facts_and_stats/history.php. [Accessed 11 12 2017].

ABOUT THE AUTHOR

Philip Shelper has over 13 years' experience within the loyalty industry, including roles at Qantas Frequent Flyer and Vodafone, as well as running his own loyalty management consultancy, Loyalty & Reward Co, which he established in 2013. Loyalty & Reward Co focuses on loyalty program design and implementation for major companies globally.

Phil is a member of hundreds of loyalty programs, and a researcher of loyalty psychology and loyalty history, all of which he uses to understand the essential dynamics of what makes a successful loyalty program.

He is an active cryptocurrency trader and presents regularly on blockchain loyalty at conferences and meet-ups around the world.

Phil is always interested to share knowledge about blockchain loyalty, and regularly does so via *www.blockchainloyalty.io*, a global blockchain loyalty resource centre.

Connect with Phil via:
Linked In: *www.linkedin.com/in/philipshelper*
Twitter: @phil_shelper
Loyalty & Reward Co: *www.rewardco.com.au*

ACKNOWLEDGEMENTS

Thank you to the following people for their help in the creation of this book and for supporting my journey into the world of blockchain loyalty:

My wife, Kate Ireland, for her insights into Egyptology and neo-tribalism.

Lincoln Hunter, Principal of Loyalty Legal, the best loyalty industry legal firm on the planet (*www.loyaltylegal.com.au*).

Andrew Lowe, MD PiCoLabs, (*www.picolabs.co*) and respected partner for the UNSW research project.

Tony Nguyen, CTO PiCoLabs.

Alexis (Lexi) Whelan.

The following individuals at Piper Alderman who made valuable contributions to Chapter 5 written by Mr Michael Bacina (Partner):

Mr Will Fennell (Partner)

Mr Tom Skevington (Lawyer)

Ms Louisa Xu (Lawyer)

Mr Petros Xenos (Law Clerk)

The following people from UNSW for their tireless support of the UNSW research project:

Professor Salil S. Kanhere, UNSW School of Computer Science and Engineering

Professor Ron Van der Meyden, UNSW School of Computer Science and Engineering

Senior Lecturer Eric Lim, UNSW School of Information Systems and Technology Management

Daniel Bar, bitfwd (*www.bitfwd.com*)

Danielle Neale, UNSW Engineering

The team from Loyalty Corp (*www.loyaltycorp.com.au*) for their generous support in providing the platform solution for the UNSW research project:

Andrew Kallen

Nathan Sceberras

Pavel Zagaria

Brad Mathews

Max Savransky, Loyalty Director, Loyalty & Reward Co (*www.rewardco.com.au*).

Stacey Lyons, Marketing Director, Loyalty & Reward Co (*www.rewardco.com.au*).

Tom Goldenberg, 3radical (*www.3radical.com*), for giving me a stage to talk blockchain loyalty.

David Feldman, for turning me on to loyalty psychology.

Pat and Tony Shelper, my crazy, awesome parents.

CPSIA information can be obtained
at www.ICGtesting.com
Printed in the USA
LVHW021452310323
743154LV00028B/705

9 780648 353539